ADVENTURES ALONG BORDERS

ADVENTURES AMONG BORDERS

ADVENTURES ALONG BORDERS
Personal Reminiscences

Graeme S. Mount

BLACK
ROSE
BOOKS

Montreal/New York/London

Black Rose Books No. NN367

National Library of Canada Cataloguing in Publication Data

Mount, Graeme S. (Graeme Stewart), 1939–

Adventures along borders : personal reminiscences / Graeme S. Mount

ISBN 978-1-55164-325-0 (bound) ISBN 978-1-55164-324-3 (pbk.)

1. Mount, Graeme S. (Graeme Stewart), 1939– --Travel. 2. Voyages and travels. 3. Boundaries. 4. History, Modern--20th century. 5. History, Modern--21st century. I. Title.

G465.M6888 2008   910.4   C2008-905058-4

C.P. 1258	2250 Military Road	99 Wallis Road
Succ. Place du Parc	Tonawanda, NY	London, E9 5LN
Montréal, H2X 4A7	14150	England
Canada	USA	UK

To order books:

In Canada: (phone) 1-800-565-9523 (fax) 1-800-221-9985
email: utpbooks@utpress.utoronto.ca

In the United States: (phone) 1-800-283-3572 (fax) 1-800-351-5073

In the UK & Europe: (phone) 44 (0)20 8986-4854 (fax) 44 (0)20 8533-5821
email: order@centralbooks.com

Our Web Site address: http://www.blackrosebooks.net

Printed in Canada

Table of Contents

SECTION 1: MAKING BORDERS

SECTION II: ENFORCING BORDERS

Land Borders Crossed (in chronological order)

Canada/USA (often)

Netherlands/Germany (1961, 1989, 2000)

Germany/Austria (1961, 1989)

Austria/Yugoslavia (1961)

Yugoslavia/Greece (1961)

Italy/Vatican (1961)

Italy/Switzerland (1961)

Switzerland/France (1961, 1986, 1992)

USA/Mexico (1963, 1966, 1982)

Venezuela/Colombia (1970)

Guyana/Brazil (1974)

Guatemala/Honduras (1977)

Yugoslavia/Romania (1980)

Spain/France (1986, 1989, 1990)

Switzerland/Liechtenstein (1986)

Spain/Andorra (1986)

Brazil/Paraguay (1988)

Brazil/Argentina (1988)

Netherlands/Belgium (1989)

Belgium/Luxembourg (1989, 1990)

West Germany/East Germany (1989)

Austria/Hungary (1989)

Austria/Switzerland (1990)

United Kingdom/Ireland (1989, 2006)

France/Monaco (1990)

Thailand/Malaysia (1991)

Germany/Luxembourg (1992)

Germany/Switzerland (1992)

Chile/Argentina (1997)

Sweden/Norway (2000)

Portugal/Spain (2001)

Costa Rica/Panama (2004, 2005)

Thailand/Cambodia (2008)

Land Borders Visited but not Crossed (in chronological order)

(Author visited the first named)

Israel/Jordan (1961)

Israel/Syria (1961)

Israel/Lebanon (1961)

Guatemala/Belize (1978)

Yugoslavia/Albania (1980)

Zimbabwe/Zambia (1990)

Zimbabwe/Mozambique (1990)

South Korea/North Korea (1999)

Macau/People's Republic of China (1999)

Germany/Poland (2000)

East Timor/Indonesia (2006)

China/North Korea (2006)

Laos/Thailand (2007)

Hong Kong/People's Republic of China (1999 and 2008)

Introduction

Almost every Canadian has a story about an experience at a border-crossing, most often the one between Canada and the United States. In the case of my own nuclear family, the most memorable was probably one from Turner, Montana, to Climax, Saskatchewan, late in August 1982. I was beginning my second sabbatical as a member of the History Department of Laurentian University in Sudbury, Ontario. Sudbury is home to many French-Canadians, and I was curious to see to what extent American citizens of Spanish or Mexican extraction had adapted to life in the United States after the Mexican War of 1846–1848. As a result of that war, the United States annexed what had been Mexico's northwest and inherited the people who lived in such places as New Mexico and California. My wife (Joan) and my sons (Fraser, age 10, and Andrew, age 4) spent most of June, July, and August in Santa Fe, the New Mexican capital, where I frequented the State Archives and interviewed people. We decided to return home by driving due north to Saskatchewan, so that we could visit friends in Eastend, where Joan and I had lived some years earlier.

There were no exit controls at Turner, but the woman on duty in Climax interrogated us for forty-five minutes. We were undoubtedly the most exotic people whom she had seen in some time. "What were you doing in the United States, and how long were you there?" she asked. These were routine questions for any customs officer to ask returning Canadians.

"Since the beginning of June," I replied. "We crossed the border at Sault Ste. Marie June 2nd, and I have been researching the history of Spanish-Americans and Mexican-Americans in Santa Fe, New Mexico, since then."

"Why are you crossing the border *here*?" she demanded. She had noticed the Ontario plates on our car and wondered why people from Ontario were returning via a triangular route instead of along a straight southwest to northeast line that would have taken us to Sault Ste. Marie, Detroit/Windsor, or Buffalo/Fort Erie. I replied that we planned to visit friends in Eastend.

"What friends in Eastend?" she snarled. The population of southwestern Saskatchewan was so small that people from Climax frequently met people from Eastend, almost two hours of driving to the northwest, at curling bonspiels, church activities, bingos, or fairs. I gave her the names of people whom we expected to see, and she changed the topic.

"What is the value of your purchases in the United States?" she continued. I gave a round number well below the legal limit. At the time, the Canadian dollar was worth considerably less than the American, and as a professor on sabbatical, I was earning less than my usual salary. Also, this was far from our first trip to the United States. There had been many other opportunities for shopping there.

"Exactly that amount?" she repeated suspiciously. Of course I had given only an educated guess, an approximate amount.

As nobody else was driving from Turner to Climax at the time, the customs officer could (and did) focus on us. Although she never left her booth to inspect the car, she insisted upon a complete list of purchases. Whenever I mentioned something, she asked, "Anything else?" We reached the point where I mentioned that I was taking into Canada toothpaste purchased in Santa Fe.

"How much of the tube did you use while you were in the United States?" she asked.

"Two-thirds," I replied. "One-third of the tube is left."

"How much did you pay for the tube of toothpaste?" she said. Either I remembered or gave a credible estimate.

"You paid $3 for a tube of toothpaste," she calculated. "You used two-thirds of it. Therefore you are importing into Canada $1 worth of toothpaste." She added that to her list.

When she was satisfied that the list was complete, the customs officer added the figures, right to the cent. Giving me the sum of the expenditures, she then had another question. "Is that in Canadian or in American dollars?"

"American," I answered. After all, we had been deep inside the United States, where most people would not have recognized Canadian money if they had seen it.

She calculated again and decided that we were still within the legal limit. "You can go now," she finally said, "but in future, whenever you visit the United States, keep track of *every* expenditure." As we drove north from Climax, I fully expected that she would have alerted the RCMP to intercept us near Shaunavon, where the north-south highway from Climax to the Trans-Canada intersected with Saskatchewan's east-west Highway 13, which would take us to Eastend, but that did not happen. We were home free. We had crossed the border many times before then and have crossed the border many times since then, but her interrogation was unique. Nor, despite her admonition, did we record trivial purchases such as toothpaste on subsequent trips, and no customs officer whom we have encountered since August 1982 has asked such detailed questions.

Our reaction to the Climax experience ranged from amazement to amusement, but we are well aware of our good fortune. As Canadians, we can cross more borders with less red tape and fewer reasons to fear than can most people. Also, as we know from experience, border crossings from Canada into any of the neighbours—the United States, St. Pierre et Miquelon (French territory), and Greenland (Danish territory)—are usually routine. Especially since the events of 11 September 2001, some officers ask more questions than others, but as long as we arrive with the right documents, the time at the customs booth is no more than a matter of a few minutes, if that.

Elsewhere life is not so simple, even for Canadians. Some international border crossings have been, or remain, much more interesting, even challenging, than any of Canada's. The ones to be mentioned here, in chronological order of our experience, are those of the former Yugoslavia months after the death of Josip Broz Tito (1980); the one between Brazil and Argentina (1988); the inter-German border (August 1989, three months before the opening of the Berlin Wall); the iron curtain between Austria and Hungary (1989); the inter-Irish border (1989); the border between Zimbabwe and Mozambique (1990); that between Argentina and Chile (1997); North Korea's borders with South Korea (1999) and with the People's Republic of China (2006); the maritimes borders between Trinidad and Venezuela and between Tobago and Barbados (2004); the Thai/Cambodian border (2008); the border between Hong Kong and the People's Republic of China (2008). Perhaps Canadians who read about these situations will appreciate the relative ease of travel which we enjoy. We may even come to appreciate the work of Canada Customs, which prevents the free flow of illicit drugs and weapons even as it delays us and charges duty on our purchases.

In many ways, borders have become sacred. When in 1990 Iraqi President Saddam Hussein sent his army across the border and annexed Kuwait, a full member of the United Nations, the Security Council deemed such actions intolerable, and authorized the use of force to expel the Iraqi army from Kuwait. Early in March 2008, the Colombian Army pursued insurgents from the rebel group FARC (*Fuerzas Armadas de la Revolución Colombiana*; Armed Forces of the Colombian Revolution) across the border into Ecuador and killed a FARC leader. The government of Colombian President Álvaro Uribe justified the attack on the grounds that Ecuador was unjustifiably tolerant of FARC, but Ecuadorean President Rafael Correa denied the accusation. He claimed that his country had become a victim of Colombia's civil war. Venezuelan President Hugo Chávez claimed that the Colombian President was a criminal, and both Correa and Chávez sent thousands of soldiers to their respective borders with Colombia in order to deter what they claimed was a Colombian predator. Happily, the South American crisis ended as quickly as it had begun. The three Presidents met in Santo Domingo, neutral territory, and on 7 March resolved their differences. Amid a series of *abrazos* (hugs), President Uribe promised that Colombia would respect its neighbours' sovereignty, and President Correa called for international forces to patrol his country's border with strife-torn Colombia.[1]

In April 2008, Presidents of countries in southern Africa proved reluctant to reprimand or chastise Zimbabwean President Robert Mugabe for governing his country in a thuggish and destructive manner, or for concealing election returns which were not what he wanted. As long as Mugabe limited his thuggish and destructive activities to his own country and his own people, the other Presidents were prepared to be tolerant—even if such tolerance reflected badly on themselves and on Africans as a whole in the eyes of outside investors.

This book divides into two sections. Section I, Making Borders (Chapters 1–4), deals with the history of borders in general and with three fairly recent attempts to establish borders: Chile's in Antarctica, Iceland's fishing limits in the North Atlantic, and the maritime boundaries of the Caribbean nation formally known as Trinidad and Tobago. That section should appeal to readers with an interest in history and current events. Section II, Enforcing Borders (Chapters 5–14), deals with personal anecdotes of my experiences and those of my wife at borders. It should entertain anyone who has crossed a border and who contemplates crossing one—in other words, most of us.

Note

1. Reconstructed from a Deutsche Welle TV newscast heard in Kunming, China, noon (Chinese time), 8 March 2008.

To friends and family members
who have travelled with me and made these stories possible
and to Laurentian University
which gave me a mandate to roam the world.

PHOTOGRAPHS

The Canada-U.S. border between Quebec's Eastern Townships and Vermont is an artificial line modified in 1842 to correct a surveyor's mistake. Here the author's young son Andrew poses beside a boundary marker at Rock Island, Quebec/Derby Line, Vermont. In July 2008, the U.S. border patrol shot three Brazilians who were attempting an illegal entry at this point. Photographed by the author, 1983.

Undoubtedly the most spectacular views along the Canada-US border is the Detroit skyline as seen from Windsor, Ontario. Photographed by the author, 1984.

In 1974, Guyana's relations with neighbouring Venezuela were tense as Venezuela claimed more than half Guyana's territory. Although relations with Brazil were much better, the Guyana Defence Force (Army) had troops along the otherwise unoccupied land next to the Brazilian border in order to reconfirm Guyana's claim. Photographed by the author, February 1974.

In 1974, small craft were the only means of transportation across the Orinduik River between Guyana and Brazil. Photographed by the author, February 1974.

Brazilians *did* inhabit their side of the border in 1974, but living conditions were rudimentary. Photographed by the author, February 1974.

Rivers often provide international boundaries, and some of those rivers have spectacular waterfalls. Here (left to right) Rupert and Elisabeth Cook, Joan and Graeme Mount, stand on the Brazilian side of Iguazú Falls (known as "Iguaçu" in Portuguese-speaking Brazil), February 1988. In the background is Argentina. Taken by a Japanese tourist.

An election poster greets new arrivals at Puerto Presidente Stroessner, Paraguay. The previous Sunday, President Alfredo Stroessner had "won" his eighth consecutive presidential election. Only one year into his five-year term, Stroessner was ousted in a 1989 coup d'état, and Puerto Presidente Stroessner became Puerto del Este. Photographed by the author, 19 February 1988.

Metres from the Tancredo Neves Bridge between Brazil and Argentina, Argentine authorities remind the world that the Falkland Islands (called the Malvinas by Argentina) belong to Argentina, not to the United Kingdom which had regained them in a war fought only six years earlier. Photographed by the author, February 1988.

After Argentina and Chile defined their border on Tierra del Fuego in 1881, Argentine authorities wanted Argentines to move there in order to anchor the claim. As most found the area too cold and too remote, in 1896 the government opened a penal colony at Ushuaia, now the world's most southerly city. The prison closed in 1947, but Ushuaia survived and is now the departure point for cruises to Antarctica. Taken by the author inside the prison at Ushuaia, March 2009

After the Great Wall of China, the world's oldest artificial boundary marker is probably Hadrian's Wall, which separated Roman Britain (now England) from less controllable areas north of the Solway Firth in the west to the Tyne estuary in the east. Photographed by the author, 1986.

Pro-republican graffiti appeared on walls of buildings in the Roman Catholic section of the Northern Ireland border town, Strabane. Here, an arm draped in the colours of the Tricolour flag of the Republic of Ireland disposes of the Union Jack. Photographed by the author, October 1989.

Berlin's Brandenburg Gate and the Berlin Wall were symbols of the Cold War from August 1961 until November1989. The Brandenburg gate stood behind the Wall in East Berlin. In the foreground, a sign warned "Attention! You are now leaving West Berlin." Photographed by the author, August 1989.

Crosses opposite the Wall recall those killed by East German border guards while trying to cross illegally from East Berlin to West Berlin between 1961 and 1989. Photographed by the author in August 1989.

Another Cold War marker was Berlin's Checkpoint Charlie, the only crossing point for vehicular traffic during the life of the Wall. Photographed by the author, August 1989.

The Strassebahn (S-Bahn or elevated railway) provided a link between West Berlin and the Friedrichstrasse station in East Berlin, where there were border controls. Photographed by the author from West Berlin, August, 1989.

A sign warns those approaching the West Berlin shore of the River Spree not to go into the water.

(Below) Access to the shore of the River Spree from the British sector of West Berlin was easy, but barricades on the East Berlin shore (opposite) prevented anyone from jumping into the water and swimming to freedom.

Photographed by the author, August 1989.

From the S-Bahn between West Berlin and East Berlin's Friedrichstrasse Station, travellers could see that there were two Walls, with a nomansland or razed zone between the two. Note the absence of graffiti on the East Berlin side of the Wall. Photographed by the author from the S-Bahn, August 1989.

Polish shoppers return to Slubice, on the Polish side of the Oder River, after a shopping trip to trip to Frankfurt-an-der-Oder, on the German side. Since Poland joined the Schengen Agreement 21 December 2007, border controls have ended. Picture taken by the author from Frankfurt-an-der-Oder, August 2000.

Saturday afternoon traffic jams such as these were common along the Austro-Hungarian border in August 1989, as Austrian campers sought to visit Hungary's Lake Balaton. Note the number of vehicles facing the camera and awaiting clearance from Hungarian Customs and Immigration, and the much small number headed in the opposite direction, into Austria. Nowadays, both Austria and Hungary are members of the Schengen Community and traffic flows freely between them. Photographed by the author from the Austrian side, 19 August 1989.

East German campers "vacationed" by the thousands on the shores of Hungary's Lake Balaton, pictured here, in August 1989, then refused to return home. With money from the West German government as an incentive, early in September Hungarian authorities opened the border and let them drive into Austria, from where they could proceed to their new homes in West Germany. East Germany abandoned the Wall as a border control 9 November 1989, barely two months later. Photographed by the author, 22 August 1989.

Victoria Falls on the Zambezi River separates Zimbabwe (until 1964, Southern Rhodesia) from Zambia (until 1964, Northern Rhodesia), both part of the Federation of Rhodesia and Nyasaland (FRN) from 1953 until 1963. Once the Federation disintegrated, both countries established border controls. Photographed by the author, June 1990.

Pedestrians cross the bridge from Victoria Falls, Zimbabwe, and head toward Livingstone, Zambia, at a time when goods were much more plentiful in Zimbabwe than in Zambia. The reverse is now the case. Photographed by the author, June 1990.

Zimbabwe's army wanted minimal publicity for military assistance rendered to Mozambique's government during that country's civil war in 1990. The author was interrogated as a possible South African spy for taking pictures along the border in June 1990. Photographed by the author, June 1990.

The view of bustling Dandong, China, visible by day to North Korean residents of sleepy Sinuiju (*below*), taken by the author from a Chinese speedboat in the Yalu River, 4 July 2006.

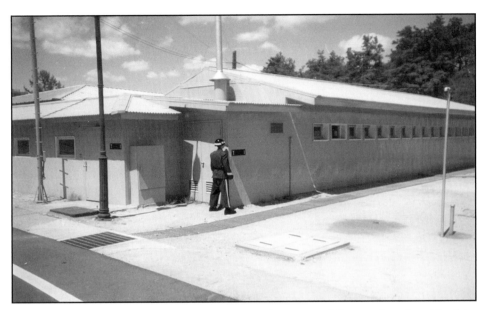

A South Korean soldier monitors activities by North Korean soldiers on the other side of the inter-Korean border, at Panmunjom, while partially shielding his body behind a building. Picture taken by the author, April 1999.

An abandoned North Korean Customs Office (left side) beside the Yalu River near Hushan, China. Access to the bridge from the Chinese side is barricaded. Picture taken by the author from the Great Wall, 5 July 2006.

Entry into the Kingdom of Cambodia at Poipet. This Cambodian border city, has many casinos, as Thailand does not have legalized gambling. In October 2008, Thai and Cambodian soldiers shot at each other at Preah Vilhear, a disputed border area to the north. Picture taken by the author, February 2008.

A train of Hong Kong's ultra-modern Kowloon Canton Railway pulls into the border station at Lok Ma Chau. Picture taken by the author, March 2008.

SECTION I
MAKING BORDERS

Chapter 1

A Brief History of International Boundary Making

International boundaries have long been a significant reality in the lives of ordinary people. One pivotal event in the evolution of international boundaries was the 1648 Treaty of Westphalia, which ended the Thirty Years War. That conflict, provoked in large measure by religious quarrels between Roman Catholics and Protestants, created such horrendous destruction of lives and property across Central Europe that European governments accepted the principle that governments could do almost anything they pleased within their own territories—as long as they remained within those territories, marked by clearly defined boundaries.[1] Countries could have different laws governing such matters as religion, education, taxation, development of resources, and public hygiene, and foreigners who did not like those laws could adapt to them or stay away.

Hitler's treatment of Jews in Nazi Germany led to some modification of the Westphalian principles. On 10 December 1948, the United Nations General Assembly adopted a Universal Declaration of Human Rights, serious violators of which have sometimes suffered consequences. Following the disintegration of Yugoslavia in 1991, United Nations forces intervened (not always effectively) to protect minorities within the former Yugoslavia: Muslims in Bosnia, ethnic Albanians in Kosovo, ethnic Serbs in Croatia. Indeed, the 1993 Battle of Medak Pocket between Canadian and Croatian soldiers in defence of the rights of ethnic Serbs was the Canadian Army's most serious engagement between the end of the Korean War in 1953 and the 21st century commitment in Afghanistan.[2] The United Nations acted, albeit ineffectively, to protect Rwanda's Tutsis from its Hutus,[3] and it is now attempting to protect Sudanese in the Darfur region. At time of writing (spring 2008), the United Nations is taking action to prosecute leaders in Cambodia's Khmer Rouge government (1975-1979) whose policies and actions cost the lives of 20 per cent of the Cambodian people.[4] Nevertheless, governments retain considerable freedom to make their own laws and govern according to their wishes within their own territory.

While lawmakers accepted the principle that different countries could have different laws, governments wanted defensible boundaries so that no other country could impose its laws upon one or more unwilling neighbours. Events in Europe between 1914 and 1919, between 1937 and 1945, and again in the early 1990s, confirm that boundaries are subject to change. Accordingly, security concerns have been an important factor in the location of boundaries. Since 1648, with the exception of Gibraltar, the United Kingdom has made no claims on the European mainland. The North Sea and the English Channel effectively protected the British people from such predators as Napoleon I in the 19th century and Hitler in the 20th. Napoleon III, Emperor of France between 1852 and 1870, wanted defensible boundaries—waterways and mountain ranges—for his country. Many of those boundaries were already in place. The English Channel, the Bay of Biscay, and the Mediterranean offered protection from naval invasion. The wide and rapidly flowing Rhine could deter invaders from the east, the Pyrenees from the south. Napoleon III regarded France's southeast as its most vulnerable frontier and resolved that problem by assisting Italy to acquire lands from the Austro-Hungarian Empire. In return, France received the Alpes Maritimes region (the area around Nice and Menton) of what would have been Italy. There are no quarrels about land boundaries of Iceland or of the Caribbean nation of Trinidad and Tobago, but such challenges as the development of modern technology and the world's insatiable appetite for fish have led both to develop Coast Guards in order to protect their interests.

Security concerns have led not only to defensible boundaries but to the creation and preservation of buffer states. When Belgium separated from The Netherlands in 1830, authorities in the United Kingdom and Prussia were determined that despite its French-speaking population, Belgium must not become a part of France. France already was sufficiently large as to pose a security threat to the United Kingdom and Prussia. Fortunately, the French government agreed to a separate and independent Belgium, but the 1914 invasion of Belgium by Germany, Prussia's successor state, prompted British intervention into what became World War I. Similarly in South America, Uruguay emerged as a buffer state between Argentina and Brazil. Like Argentines, Uruguayans spoke (and continue to speak) Spanish. Brazilians spoke (and continue to speak) Portuguese. The mighty Río de la Plata could provide a defensible boundary for both Brazil and Argentina, South America's two largest countries, but that would have left the Uruguayans within a country which to them was alien. The presence of the Argentine army across a land frontier was too close to the Brazilian heartland for comfort. After war over the issue between 1825 and 1828, the governments of Argentina and Brazil agreed to resolve the dispute by accepting an independent Uruguay. Ian Smith, the Rhodesian Prime Minister who defied most of the world with a Unilateral Declaration of Independence in 1965, told the author during an interview in 1990 that South African authorities initially supported his government because the mighty Zambezi River (between black African-ruled Zambia and European settler-dominated Rhodesia, now Zimbabwe) was a more effective barrier than the Limpopo (the river which forms the border between Rhodesia/Zimbabwe and South Africa, where only people of European extraction had the right to vote and govern before 1994).

Empires rise and fall, and their demise creates a new set of problems. Europe required centuries to recover from the collapse of the Roman Empire. Current problems in the Balkans and the Middle East are attributable in large measure to the Ottoman Empire and its disappearance. British weakness in 1922 permitted an independent Ireland, but the location of the British-Irish boundary has remained a contentious issue. In 1885, European diplomats met in Berlin, where they divided the African continent. African boundaries would reflect European interests—acquisition of desired resources, including land for settlers from the homeland; the use of Belgian and Portuguese colonies to separate Europe's great powers from one another. Negotiators in Berlin paid little attention to such African realities as language, religious differences, or distribution of resources. Since they regained independence in the second half of the 20th century, Africans have feared to set precedents by changing those colonial boundaries, despite their questionable origins and uncertain or improbable viability.

One of the world's least permeable borders must be the land boundary between North and South Korea. During the Russo-Japanese War of 1904-1905, Japanese forces occupied Korea. In 1910, Japan annexed Korea outright. In 1945, as the Japanese Empire was collapsing, the Soviet and U.S. Armies had to determine which territories each would occupy. Otherwise, the victorious Allies might have found themselves fighting each other. Colonel Dean Rusk and Colonel Charles Bonesteel of the United States Army—appointed to suggest a demarcation line north of which Japanese forces would surrender to the Soviets, south of which to the United States—found no acceptable mountain ranges or rivers but settled upon the 38th parallel, the first one north of Korea's capital, Seoul. By that point, the Soviet Army had captured Berlin, Bucharest, Budapest, Prague, Sofia, Vienna, and Warsaw, and the two U.S. officers wanted a capital city which the U.S. Army could occupy. Soviet authorities accepted the Rusk-Bonesteel proposal.[5] In 1948, American and Soviet authorities established separate governments in North and South Korea. In 1950, Communist North Korea crossed the 38th parallel and invaded South Korea. Sixteen members of the United Nations sent forces to resist North Korean aggression by assisting South Korea, and when soldiers of the United Nations Command (Americans) approached the Yalu River separating North Korea from the People's Republic of China, Chinese soldiers went to the assistance of North Korea. One condition of the 1953 Armistice Agreement was that South Korea must have more defensible borders, not simply an imaginary line like the 38th parallel.[6]

Another Cold War border, happily no longer in existence, was that between East and West Germany. Hitler's Germany had inflicted such devastation upon the Soviet Union, killing perhaps five per cent of the total population and further impoverishing the survivors, that Soviet leaders wanted to protect their homeland from further German or Western European attacks. There were no formidable mountain ranges or salt water barriers between the Soviet Union and the most formidable Western European countries, and the Soviet solution was to annex, occupy, or sustain Soviet-friendly governments in the countries located between the Soviet Union and Germany, as well as in a portion of Germany itself. Disagreements among the occupiers of Germany—the United States, the United Kingdom, France on the one hand, and the Soviet Union on the other—led to the decades- long partition of that country. Areas occupied by the three Western powers would form the Federal Republic of Germany, West Germany; the Soviet-occu- pied zone would become the German Democratic Republic, East Germany. Berlin, Germany's capital, would be a separate entity. During World War II, the future occupiers agreed that each should occupy and control a sector of Berlin in order to facilitate the government of Germany as a whole. The Soviet sector of Berlin—known in the West as East Berlin—became capital of East Germany, while the three Western sectors became West Berlin. Communist East Germany surrounded West Berlin on all sides. West Germany and West Berlin benefitted from the Marshall Plan, which enabled the recovery of Western European economies. East Germany paid reparations to the Soviet Union as compensation for damages inflicted during World War II. West Germany and West Berlin grew rich as East Germany stagnated, even regressed. Under the circumstances, millions of East Germans fled, usually from East Berlin to West Berlin, where until the summer of 1961 escape was a simple matter of riding the subway or S-Bahn (*Strassebahn* or street railway, an elevated railway) or crossing the street. Had the exodus continued, East Germany would have ceased to be viable, and once East German leaders persuaded their Soviet sponsors to allow them to build a Wall to block such traffic, the Wall appeared.[6] It remained in place from August 1961 until November 1989. Chapter 7 reviews a train ride from West Germany across East German territory to West Berlin and life on either side of the Berlin Wall in the summer of 1989.

Boundaries have also emerged for other reasons. The basic boundary between the United States and what is now Canada emerged almost in a state of absentmindeness. The chief British negotiator, Richard Oswald, was a businessman who wanted peace at any price so that he and his friends could proceed with the serious business of making money. A fortuitious British military victory at Gibraltar stiffened the demands of his employer.[8] U.S. President James Knox Polk (1845-1949) wanted salt water ports on the Pacific Ocean and to that end annexed California, which had been Mexican, and the lands around Puget Sound (now part of the State of Washington), which had been in dispute between the United Kingdom and the United States. He also annexed the lands between what had been the westernmost territories of the United States and the newly acquired ports, at the same time leaving the lands heavily populated by Mexicans outside the United States. Polk's contemporaries, if not Polk himself, wanted a maximum of land and a minimum of Mexicans.[9] The purpose behind the location of the inter-Irish border was to permit the pro-British Protestants of the Belfast area to outvote as many Roman Catholics, Irish nationalists, as possible. Had Northern Ireland been limited to areas with Protestant majorities, it would have been smaller; had it included all nine counties of Ulster, instead of only six, Protestants could not have retained control.[10] Yugoslavia's pre-1991 boundaries reflected the ambitions of the Serbian King, an ally of the World War I victors. Similarly, Romania gained Transylvania from Hungary, which had fought on the losing side of that conflict, but the presence of ethnic German and Hungarian minorities kept the spirit of irridentism alive, at least in Hungary.[11] Latin American land boundaries reflect Spanish and Portuguese colonial boundaries, modified by conflict. However, ambiguities leading to conflicts and potential conflicts arose because colonial authorities had not been clear about the limits of intra-empire borders on largely unpopulated deserts and in totally unpopulated parts of high mountain ranges. Late 20th century technological developments created a need for maritime boundaries, in the Caribbean as in the Canadian Arctic.

Boundaries probably predate the human race. Wolves and their relatives, dogs, certainly have a sense of territorial ownership. Most readers will remember occasions when they were walking along a sidewalk and a dog barked or charged. Once the pedestrian(s) had passed what the dog considered to be his territory, the dog retreated. The Qin Dynasty which governed China from 221-206 B.C. defined that empire's northern boundary with the famous Great Wall of China. Apart from the Biblical Jordan River, the best known boundary in the West prior to 1648 was probably the northern frontier of the Roman Empire: Hadrian's Wall across the neck of England, south of Scotland; and the formidable Rhine and Danube Rivers (except for Romania north of the Danube). Boundaries are facts of life, in place for historic reasons. People must and do adapt to them, for they are not going to disappear.

It is true that some border controls are vanishing, but the borders themselves remain. On 5 September 1944, the exiled, London-based governments of Belgium, The Netherlands, and Luxembourg agreed to a Customs Union, which became effective in 1948. None of those governments surrendered territory. However, they agreed on common rules regarding anyone or anything which would enter *any* of the three Benelux countries, as they were known, along with free movement of goods and people once they were inside the Customs Union. In 1985 and 1990, the Benelux countries, France, and West Germany adopted two Schengen Agreements, named for the Dutch community where they were signed. Schengen effectively expanded the Benelux Customs Union to include France and Germany. The inter-German border disappeared with East Germany 3 October 1990, one of the few international borders actually to vanish since 1945. Between 1990 and 21 December 2007, most countries of continental Europe joined the Schengen Customs Union. Even Iceland, Norway, and Switzerland—all of which remain outside the European Union—have ageed to Schengen, and Romania and

Bulgaria will soon join. This means that from Estonia to Portugal, from Italy to Norway and Iceland, from the Bay of Biscay to the River Bug between Poland and Belarus, there is free movement of people and goods.

However, border controls remain, even in the First World. Schengen countries maintain common rules to be enforced against arrivals from outside the Schengen area. The United Kingdom and the Republic of Ireland have a Customs Union of their own, but they are not part of Schengen, nor are people from other continents, Albanians, nor citizens of countries which were once part of the Soviet Union, nor—with the exception of Slovenia—citizens of countries which were once part of Yugoslavia. Border controls remain between, for example, Serbia and Hungary (a Schengen country), not to mention between non-Schengen Serbia and non-Schengen Croatia, where before 1991 there were none. Greeks need not pass through Customs and Immigration when travelling to Italy, but Albanians must do so. Schengen is unique, with no counterparts outside Europe. Since the events of 11 September 2001, controls along the Canada-U.S. and Mexico-U.S. borders have grown steadily tighter. In Asia, the Thai-Cambodian border, closed in the era of the notorious Khmer Rouge (1975-1979) has re-opened, but as indicated in Chapter 12, it still presents challenges.

Note

1. Religion was by no means the only cause of the Thirty Years War, but it was an important factor. See Peter H. Wilson, "Dynasty, Constitution, and Confession: The Role of Religion in the Thirty-Years War," *International History Review*, XXX, 3 (Sept. 2008), pp. 473-514.

2. Carol Off, *The Ghosts of Medak Pocket: The Story of Canada's Secret War* (Toronto: Random House Canada, 2004). See also Timothy Garten Ash, *History of the Present: Essays, Sketches, and Dispatches from Europe in the 1990s* (New York: Random House, 1990), pp. 274-369; Martin Gilbert, *A History of the Twentieth Century*, III (Toronto: Stoddard, 1999), selected passages from pp. 722-907; Tony Judt, *Postwar: A History of Europe since 1945* (New York: Penguin, 2005), pp. 665-685.

3. Roméo Dallaire, *Shake Hands with the Devil* (Toronto: Random House Canada, 2003).

4. See below, Chapter 12.

5. Dean Rusk, *As I Saw It* (New York: W.W. Norton, 1990), 119-120, 123-124.

6. Graeme S. Mount, *The Diplomacy of War: The Case of Korea* (Montreal: Black Rose Press, 2004), p. 123.

7. Hope M. Harrison, *Driving the Soviets Up the Wall* (Princeton: Princeton University Press, 2003).

8. A.L. Burt, *The United States, Great Britain and British North America from the Revolution to the Establishment of Peace after the War of 1812* (Toronto: Ryerson, 1940).

9. Norman Graebner, *Empire on the Pacific: A Study in American Continental Expansion* (New York: Ronald Press, 1955).

10. John Darby (editor), *Northern Ireland: The Background to the Conflict* (Belfast: Appletree Press, 1983); David Harkness, *Northern Ireland since 1920* (Dublin: Helicon, 1983); Thomas Hennessey, *A History of Northern Ireland* (New York: St. Martin's Press, 1997); Derek Lundy, *The Bloody Red Hand: A Journey through Truth, Myth and Terror in Northern Ireland* (Toronto: Alfred A. Knopf Canada, 2006); Lawrence J. McCaffrey, *Ireland: From Colony to Nation State* (Englewood Cliffs, New Jersey: Prentice Hall, 1979); John A. Murphy, *Ireland in the Twentieth Century* (Dublin: Gill and Macmillan, 1989).

11. Margaret Macmillan, *Paris, 1919* (New York: Random House, 2001-2002), pp109-135.. Also, in August 1989, the author visited Budapest, where the Communist government had agreed to multi-party elections. One of the parties displayed a map of Hungary's "lost" territories.

Chapter 2

The Role of the Chilean Navy in Territorial Expansion

Chile is by no means unique for its emphasis on its Navy as a key part of its national identity. One need think only of the United Kingdom, where the names of Elizabethan sea dogs and Admiral Nelson are household words. Nevertheless, Chileans fondly remember their Navy as a nation-builder, and with good reason. Even in the 21st century, the location of Chile's borders can be controversial, but the Chilean navy has played a vital role in establishing the claims.

Thomas Cochrane

One of the principal founders of the Chilean Navy was a Scot, Thomas Cochrane (1775-1860), 10th Earl of Dundonald, whose statue stands alongside those of Queen Isabela and Christopher Columbus on the waterfront of Valparaíso, the country's largest port. South of Santiago in Chile's Tenth District, three forts stand at the point where the Valdivia and Calle Calle Rivers empty into the Pacific. San Sebastian de la Cruz at Corral once had a Spanish garrison of 200. In 1820, Lord Cochrane fought a naval battle commemorated there and terminated Spanish rule in the area. At the time, Valdivia was Chile's southernmost port, the first South American port after rounding the Cape. As Chile then had no naval tradition, Cochrane launched a highly successful recruiting campaign in the United Kingdom and the United States. During his four-year stay in and off Chile, Cochrane became a Chilean citizen and commander-in-chief of the Chilean Navy, with the rank of Vice-Admiral. Osorno, an inland city immediately south of Valdivia on Chile's north-south highway, has a street named in

Cochrane's honour. On the mainland south of Puerto Montt, capital of the Tenth District, is a community named Cochrane. Cochrane was a veteran of the Royal Navy's fight against Napoleon before he went to Chile. Then, mission accomplished, he assisted Brazilians and Greeks in their wars of independence. Cochrane's reputation in the United Kingdom was controversial, but to Chileans he remains a hero, one who played a major role in the liberation of their national heartland.[1]

The *Ancud*

The most northerly town on the Chilean island of Chiloë, two hours south of Puerto Montt by bus, is Ancud. Outside Ancud's museum stands a replica of the ship, the *Ancud*. According to its caption,

> The schooner *Ancud*, constructed here by hand and with wood from Chiloë, sailed from this port May 22, 1843 in pursuit of its mission.
>
> After four months of fearsome navigation, on September 21 it arrived at the Strait of Magellan, where the intrepid sailors from the "Large Island" landed and raised the national flag. In the name of the government they took possession of these latitudes for Chile.
>
> This act preceded by only 24 hours the arrival of the French corvette *Phaeton*, which the very next day anchored next to the *Ancud*.

Identified as the top three officials aboard the *Ancud* were Captain John WILLIAMS Wilson, Lieutenant Manuel GÓNZALEZ Hidalgo, and Navigator Carlos MULLER. Horacio WILLIAMS, son of John, was also there. The Chilean community of Puerto Williams on Tierra del Fuego is named for John WILLIAMS.

In the United States, diplomacy (as in the cases of the Louisiana Purchase and Alaska),the army (as in the case of the Mexican Cession), and intrigue (as in the cases of Florida and Hawaii) are the most common explanations of the nation's territorial expansion. In the case of Tierra del Fuego, Chileans attribute success to their navy.

The War of the Pacific

Heroes of Chile's war against Peru and Bolivia (1779-1883) share centre-stage with those of the War of Independence in Chilean mythology. As a result of that war, Chile expanded its boundaries to deprive Bolivia of its coastline on the Pacific and rendered it a land-locked country. At the same time, Chile annexed mineral-rich land in what had been the Peruvian south. Tensions from that war had long-term consequences. When Chile proved reluctant in 1942 to sever diplomatic relations with Nazi Germany, Fascist Italy, and Imperial Japan, Franklin Roosevelt's government provided weaponry to Peru and Bolivia, but not to Chile. The government of President Juan Antonio Ríos capitulated.[2] In February 1997, Chile's national soccer team went to Bolivia's capital for a tournament. Because of the high altitude at La Paz, the Chilean players went there several days in advance so that they could acclimatize. According to an Associated Press report in Puerto Montt's newspaper, *El Llanquihue*, the players expressed surprise at the cordiality shown to them by Bolivians, despite a rupture in diplomatic relations since 1978. Yet, AP said that the Chilean organizers requested that their national anthem *not* be played during the opening ceremonies. Bitterness over Bolivia's losses during the 1879-1883 War of the Pacific might lead to whistling or booing if it were played.[3] Then in 1999, Peruvian President Alberto FUJIMORI—perhaps by then in a desperate attempt to make himself more popular—demanded the return of the *Huáscar*, a Peruvian navy ship captured by Chile, to Peru.[4]

Statues to heroes of the War of the Pacific, including Admiral Arturo PRAT, are ubiquitous throughout Chile, as are streets named in their honour. The most significant single reminder is the *Huáscar*, displayednear Concepción, site of Chile's principal naval base. One travels roughly half an hour by bus from the centre of Concepción, along Avenida PRAT to the naval base at Talcahuano. Talcahuano's main attraction is the Museo Huáscar, the very ship *Huáscar*, which played a major role in naval battles of 1879-1880. On May 21, 1879 off Iquique, the *Huáscar*—under the command of Peruvian Admiral Miguel Grau —fought the battle which immortalized Prat. Prat, captain of the *Esmeralda*, lost his life defending the Chilean cause, as did all but 59 of her crew of 199. On June 3, Grau wrote a letter of condolence to Prat's widow, Carmela Carvajal viuda de Prat, in which Grau praised Prat's valour. In turn, Grau died in action October 8, 1879.

On October 8, the Chilean Navy captured the *Huáscar*. Then, as a Chilean ship under the command of Captain Manuel Thomson, the *Huáscar* blockaded Arica. Thomson died in action in February 1880. Both the *Huáscar* and the *Esmeralda* were products of Laird Brothers of Birkenhead, England, purchased in 1865 when Peru and Chile were allies against Isabel II's Spain. The *Huáscar* served 13 years in the Peruvian navy, 22 in the Chilean.

Another naval hero of the War of the Pacific was John WILLIAMS Rebolledo, a squadron commander in 1879. By 1891, he had become commandant general of the Chilean Navy. WILLIAMS was son of John WILLIAMS, also known as Juan Guillermos, the British officer who sailed on the *Ancud*. The younger WILLIAMS resigned his commission during a Chilean Civil War in 1891 because of his personal support for besieged but doomed Chilean President José Manuel BALMACEDA.[5]

The repercussions of that war were global. According to naval historian Lawrence Sondhaus,

> By the end of the War of the Pacific, [Chile] had three armoured warships more formidable than any vessel in the U.S. Navy, a development that, combined with the acquisition of modern battleships by Brazil and Argentina, helped inspire the United States to lay down its first modern steel warships in 1883.[6]

Valparaíso 1890

In 1891, the U.S. government seemed to support what turned out to be the losing side in a Chilean civil war, then over-reacted when sailors of the *USS Baltimore* received rough treatment during shore leave in Valparaíso. Two died and others were injured, but Chileans thught that they deserved greater understanding than what Secretary of State James G. Blaine was willing to give. Blaine already had a bad reputation in Chile, for during an earlier term as Secretary of State (1881), he had urged the government of Chile not to annex lands seized from Peru and Bolivia during the War of the Pacific. Germany's annexation of Alsace-Lorraine after the Franco-Prussian War of 1870, he warned, had destabilized Europe, and it would not be in Chile's interest to destabilize South America. Chileans were not prepared to listen to sermons from the Secretary of State of the country which had annexed half of Mexico in 1848. What first appeared as a war threat from Washington in 1891 forced a reluctant Chilean apology, but from that apology arose the widely believed (although historically untrue) story of Lieutenant Carlos Peña. According to legend, Peña volunteered to lower the Chilean flag as an act of contrition, then immediately committed suicide. The credibility of this legend did nothing to improve the image of the United States in the eyes of Chileans.[7]

Antarctica

On 2 February 1997, Sunday's edition of the Santiago newspaper *El Mercurio,* Chile's counterpart to the *Globe and Mail,* carried an article by Oscar Pinochet DE LA BARRA, a veteran of Chile's first naval expedition to Antarctica fifty years ago that week. De la Barra reported that Chile had had a permanent presence in Antarctica since 6 February 1947. When the Chilean Navy arrived there, the commanding officer—Federico GUESALAGA Toro—said:

> As long as there is a ship which flies our flag, there will be only one
> Chile, from Arica [near the Peruvian border] to Antarctica.

According to de la Barra, in 1940 President Pedro AGUIRRE Cerda had announced Chile's claim to part of Antarctica, but he did nothing to enforce the claim. On 3 November 1946, Gabriel GONZÁLEZ Videla became President of Chile and quickly decided that he should take action. His Minister of Defence, Manuel BULNES Sanfuentes agreed.

Making the issue more pressing was a statement by U.S. Admiral Richard Byrd 12 November 1946, "The United States does not recognize territorial claims in Antarctica." He and a Norwegian-American, Finn Ronne, were then planning an expedition called "High Jump." Also, the British had had a presence in Antarctica since 1944, and Argentina was preparing to establish a claim.

The Chilean base, first called "Soberanía" ("Sovereignty")and then "Arturo PRAT," was located on Greenwich Island in the South Shetlands. Construction of the base took 45 days. Two ships were involved, the frigate *Iquique* and the transport ship *Angamos,* recently purchased from Canada.

Another *El Mercurio* article the same day on the Chilean expedition to Antarctica, "Misión en el Hielo" ("Mission on the ice"), said that the University of Chile provided the expedition with literature before the *Iquique* sailed from Punta Arenas 15 January 1947. Accompanying this article were primary sources from 1947. The government of President GONZÁLEZ based its Antarctic expedition upon "The Supreme Decree of the Foreign Ministry No. 1747 of 6 November 1940, which established the limits of Chilean sovereignty in Antarctica, which could not remain passively on paper but which must be made more concrete in the form of physical occupation of a territory inherited four centuries earlier from the Spanish crown."[8]

Miguel SERRANO, a former Chilean journalist and diplomat, embellished the account. On 16 February 1997, he wrote an insider's account for *El*

Mercurio. Serrano wrote that his friend Oscar PINOCHET de la Barra had already written an article in *El Mercurio*'s "Arts and Letters" section about the building of the Antarctic Base Prat in 1947. Serrano said that he was part of a second expedition. Other participants were Oscar Pinochet on behalf of the Chilean Foreign Ministry; Jose Miguel BARROS Franco from the architectural firm Julio Ripamonti, which had helped construct the first base[9]; a medical doctor, Lermanda; a photographer, Gerstmann; and soldiers. Together they created the army's Antarctic base, Bernardo O'Higgins. This happened late in 1947 and early 1948. There as a reporter for *El Mercurio*, Serrano kept copies of the telegrams which he had sent to *El Mercurio* when the base, also built by Julio Ripamonti, was built.

According to SERRANO, the navy did not yet believe in radar. The commander of the frigate *Covadonga* was an ex-submarine officer, Jorge Gandara Bofil. His dream was to command a submarine under the Antarctic ice.

In 1947, the United Kingdom challenged Chile's claims over territory which the UK also claimed. Chile's response was the establishment of the Bases Prat and O'Higgins. Serrano said that one of his companions was Sergio ONOFRE Jarpa, with whom, he wrote, he shared a common ideology. (Sergio ONOFRE Jarpa, later Augusto Pinochet's Minister of the Interior, has a reputation as a Nazi.)

SERRANO explained that when Krishna Menon was India's Foreign Minister, Menon proposed the internationalization of Antarctica. Menon had also made the proposal earlier, when he had been India's representative at the United Nations. As Foreign Minister, he remained enthusiastic. By then, the right-wing President of Chile, Carlos Ibáñez (1952-1958) had appointed Serrano as Chile's ambassador to India. Also involved were Ambassador Fatone of Argentina and President Eisenhower's special representative, Henry Cabot Lodge. Serrano decided to go over Menon's head to Nehru himself, and he reached the Indian Prime Minister through his daughter, Indira Gandhi, a future Prime Minister. "What we Chileans owe to this marvellous woman!" said Serrano.

SERRANO told Prime Minister Nehru that he had expected that his task in India would be to sell Chilean products and to buy jute. More important, however, was to defend Chile's honour and dream in Antarctica. A country as small as his could survive alongside the great powers only if it preserved its dreams and its honour. He then asked Nehru to withdraw from the United Nations India's proposal to internationalize the Antarctic. Nehru said that he would think about it, and that very day India withdrew its proposal from the United Nations. Henry Cabot Lodge thanked Serrano.

The thought of what Chileans had already sacrificed in the Antarctic made the idea of its loss unacceptable to Serrano. It had not been easy to establish Prat and O'Higgins, he said in *El Mercurio*.

Nowadays every Chilean weather forecast traces temperatures from Arica south until Antarctica, and in January 1997, Boy Scouts in their late teens conducted a well publicized camping expedition to Chilean Antarctica.[10] The air force transported them there, and Pepsi Cola paid many of the bills. Throughout February 1997 the Chilean media featured several additional articles on Chilean claims to and activity in Antarctica. On 9 February 1997, *El Mercurio* printed several pictures of the by then-fifty-year-old naval base in Antarctica, once Soberanía, subsequently Arturo PRAT. President GONZÁLES (1946-1952), said *El Mercurio*, had visited the base in 1948; other politicians followed. In 1997 the post office issued a stamp to commemorate the occasion.[11]

On 25 February one Flavio GÓMEZ Tepott published a letter to the editor about Antarctica in Puerto Montt's newspaper, *El Llanquihue*. (Except for Punta Arenas on the Strait of Magellan, Puerto Montt is Chile's southernmost city.) GÓMEZ reminded readers that on February 6, the Chilean Navy had celebrated 50 years of continued occupation of the Arturo PRAT Naval Base. Defence Minister Edmundo PÉREZ Yoma said: "Never before had the National Anthem been sung with such emotion." PÉREZ and the top naval commander, Admiral Jorge MARTÍNEZ Busch, attended ceremonies at the PRAT base. The transport ship *Aquiles* was there, along with icebreakers *Viel* and *Lautaro*. As a Radical, Gómez was proud that it was the Radical President Pedro AGUIRRE Cerda who formally established Chile's Antarctic claims in 1940. Another Radical, Gabriel GONZÁLEZ Videla, decided that it was not enough simply to make the claim. There had to be a physical presence, established in 1947.

El Llanquihue devoted much of its issue of 27 February to Antarctica and the role of the Chilean Navy in staking a territorial claim there. There was also a supplement "Nuestro Mar" ("Our Sea"), with two entries about Chile and Antarctica. First, the editorial noted the 50th anniversary of the Arturo PRAT Naval base there, tracing Chile's rights to the 1494 Treaty of Tordesillas between Spain and Portugal. Then, on November 6, 1940,by decree No. 1747, President Pedro AGUIRRE Cerda made the claim to 1,250,000 square kilometres of Antarctica, from 53 degrees to the South Pole.

Four nations objected. Argentina agreed that it and Chile had rights there but disliked Chile's boundaries. The U.S. and Japan objected mildly. Great Britain was so vociferous as to provoke the administration of Gabriel GONZÁLEZ Videla (1946-1952) to establish the PRAT Base, first known as Base Soberanía. President González personally visited the base, then established Base O'Higgins as an army base. The British government prepared to send the cruiser *Nigeria* from Cape Town "to honour the Chilean president when he would arrive on British Antarctic Territory." Storms delayed the *Nigeria*, which reached Antarctica only as GONZÁLEZ's ship, the *Pinto*, was returning with him to the Beagle Channel. The ceremony of unveiling the bust of Admiral PRAT took place February 17, 1948. According to *El Llanquihue*, the British replied in a "burlesque and arrogant" manner. Gonzalez offered a "passionate" defence when he addressed a crowd awaiting his return to Santiago.

An editorial that same day in *El Llanquihue* explained Antarctica's strategically and economic importance to Chile. If the Panama Canal were to close, Chile would control all traffic moving from Atlantic to Pacific. Already, Punta Arenas and Puerto Williams had become important jumping-off points for Chilean control of Antarctica. Moreover, scientific studies indicated that there might be more than 200,000,000 barrels of oil in Antarctica. Offshore there were rich fisheries.

El Llanquihue also noted that the Antarctic Treaty of December 1, 1959 froze the "status quo" in Antarctica, without saying what that was. Twelve countries signed it: Argentina, Australia, Belgium, Chile, France, Great Britain, Japan, New Zealand, Norway, South Africa, the USA, and the USSR. The life of the treaty was thirty years, renewable if nobody objected. Nobody did.

Pages 8–9 of the supplement carried black-and-white and coloured pictures of the PRAT Base, and a description of the Navy's work there. Cartography, assistance to navigation from mid-October to mid-March, and ice-breaking all reinforced Chile's claims to sovereignty, said *El Llanquihue*.[12]

Chile's claims to Antarctic, taken seriously at home, are not universally accepted. On 1 December 1959, Chile was one of twelve countries to sign The Antarctic Treaty. While the treaty governs the behaviour of the signatories on the frozen continent, pledging them to pursue "peaceful purposes only," Article IV says:

> 1. Nothing contained in the present Treaty shall be interpreted as: (a) a renunciation by any Contracting Party of previously asserted rights of or claims to territorial sovereignty in Antarctica...

> 2. No acts or activities taking place while the present Treaty is in force shall constitute a basis for asserting, supporting or denying a claim to territorial sovereignty in Antarctica or create any rights of sovereignty in Antarctica.

Since then, more than forty countries have added their signatures and ratified the Convention.

Nevertheless, notwithstanding the fact that the Antarctic Treaty freezes earlier claims to sovereignty, including that of Chile, there are precedents whereby facts change legal realities. In 1818, British and U.S. authorities agreed to disagree on the location of their North American boundary west of the Rocky Mountains. From Lake of the Woods to the Rockies, the border would be the 49th parallel. West of the Rockies, they agreed that U.S. citizens and British subjects could work and travel freely, and that nothing they did would establish a precedent for subsequent claims. Yet, the boundary settlement of 1846 coincided with post-1818 occupation. The Hudson's Bay Company established a post at Victoria south of the 49th parallel on Vancouver Island in 1843, and *all* Vancouver Island *did* in the end remain British. During the 1830s, American settlers poured into the Willamette Valley in what would become the State of Oregon, and Oregon *did* become part of the United States. No one can foresee whether a resource-hungry world will divide Antarctica into political jurisdictions, or whether, if that happens, Chile will own all, part, or none of what it has been claiming.

Conclusions

Chilean naval heroes are an integral part of the national identity. Thomas Cochrane was one of the country's founding fathers. The *Ancud* played an indispensable role in Chile's territorial expansion, as did Arturo PRAT. Memories of Secretary of State Blaine and an unhappy naval incident at Valparaíso affected Chilean attitudes toward World War II more than half a century later, and the role of the Chilean Navy in Antarctica are perhaps comparable to the role of the Canadian Navy in establishing Canadian sovereignty throughout the Northwest

Passage. Monuments, statues, and the media have maintained constant re-minders of the names of those heroes. Since independence, Chileans have an-nexed lands previously owned by Bolivia and Peru, and since World War II, they have worked actively to establish a claim from Antarctic's offshore islands to the South Pole.

Notes

1. For a biography of Thomas Cochrane, see David Cordingly, *Cochrane: The Real Master and Commander* (New York: Bloomsbury), 2007. Chapter 17 (pp. 272-295) deals with Cochrane's activities in Chile and Peru between 1818 and 1822.

2. Graeme S. Mount, *Chile and the Axis* (Montreal: Black Rose Press, 2001), pp.63-139, 148-149.

3. *El Llanquihue* (Puerto Montt), 8 February 1977.

4. Lawrence Sondhaus, *Navies in Modern World History* (London: Reaktion, 2004), p. 170.

5. Sondhaus, pp. 157-158, 160, 163, 165-166.

6. Sondhaus, p. 141.

7. For a more extensive account of Chilean foreign relations to 1933, see Mario BARROS Van Buren, *Historia Diplomática de Chile* (Santiago: Andrés Bello, 1971); and William F. Sater, *Chile and the United States* (Athens: University of Georgia Press, 1990). See also Ricardo Couyoumdjian, "En torno a la neutralidad de Chile durante la primera guerra mundial," in Walter SANCHEZ G. And Teresa PEREIRA L., *Cientocincuenta Años de Política Exterior Chilena* (Santiago: Editorial Universitaria, 1977), pp. 180-222.

8. *El Mercurio* (Santiago), 2 Feb. 1997.

9. Evidently Julio Ripamonte was not the only architectural firm at Base Soberanía. Maurice Poisson was also there.

10. *El Mercurio* (Santiago), 10 Jan. 1997. That edition of *El Mercurio* carried both the story and pictures.

11. *El Mercurio* (Santiago), 9 Feb. 1997.

12. *El Llanquihue* (Puerto Montt), 27 February 1997.

Chapter 3

The Ford Administration and the Anglo-Icelandic Cod War[1]

President Gerald Ford (9 August 1974-20 January 1977) inherited a wide range of problems which were not of his administration's making: Nixon's "Peace with Honor" in Vietnam, which was about to collapse; the aftermath of the Yom Kippur War of 1973, which had led to a scarcity of oil and higher oil prices; potential conflict between Greece and Turkey over Cyprus, which threatened NATO's southeastern flank; Cuban militancy in Angola and other parts of Africa; tensions on the Isthmus of Panama; as well as the usual concerns about the Soviet Union, the People's Republic of China, and North Korea.[2] To Ford and his Secretary of State, Henry Kissinger, the Icelandic fishery dispute was not nearly as important as any of those issues. Neither Ford nor Kissinger as much as mentions Iceland or the U.S. Air Force and Navy base at Keflavik in his memoirs.[3] Nor does Douglas Brinkley, Ford's most recent biographer.[4]

Nevertheless, the Icelandic fishery dispute was important—because one NATO ally (Iceland) was at odds with two others (West Germany and the United Kingdom). The United States was not a direct participant in the Icelandic fishery dispute and could have accepted almost any solution which was acceptable to the three NATO allies, if such existed.[5] The time and energy expended on Icelandic matters were considerably less than those on any of the other aforesaid issues. Moreover, fisheries bored Kissinger. On 12 October 1976, when State Department officials raised a similar issue—differing interpretations of the maritime boundary between Canada and the United States and the implications for the New England fishery, Kissinger replied, "It bores me to tears."[6]

What made the Icelandic situation special were the threat to NATO cohesiveness and the Keflavik base.[7]

It should be clear that in the matter of the cod fishery, Icelandic governments were acting on behalf of their country's economic self-interest, not because of unadulterated concern for the environment. A book recently published by the University of Iceland Press carries a reminder that Iceland has consistently "pursue[d] policies that directly conflict with prominent environmental norms by hunting whales [and] seals…"[8] Again with self-interest at stake, Iceland has invested heavily in alternatives to fossil fuels, of which it has almost none.[9] Thanks to extensive reserves of volcanically heated water, through such actions Icelanders could become almost self-sufficient in energy and therefore impervious to the vagaries of the world's oil and gas markets. It was actually profitable for Icelanders to be leaders in the fight against greenhouse gasses and global warming. Icelandic actions have been sensible, but they were not altruistic.

Background[10]

In 1972, the Icelandic government led by Prime Minister Ólafur Jóhannesson extended Iceland's exclusive fishing zone from 12 to 50 miles. By this time, fish and fish products accounted for 80 per cent of Icelandic exports, and while the cost of imports rose, the market value of fish declined. Iceland's fishermen caught an estimated 95 per cent of their fish within the 50-mile radius. There appears to have been no strong reaction from the Nixon administration in Washington, probably because (1) few if any Americans fished in the area; (2) Jóhannesson and his ministers did not extend Iceland's claims of *sovereignty*.

By contrast, two other NATO governments—the British and the West German—*did* react. When bilateral Anglo-Icelandic talks failed, the governments of Prime Minister Edward Heath and West German Chancellor Willy Brandt took the matter to the International Court of Justice in The Hague. Much to the disgust of Icelandic Prime Minister Jóhannesson, on 17 August 1973 the Court supported them by a margin of 14:1. The court imposed limits on what the British and Germans should take but agreed that they had every right to fish outside Iceland's 12-mile limit and instructed the Icelanders not to enforce the 50-mile limit. In his memoirs, Heath says that the Icelandic fishery was highly "lucrative."[11]

Meanwhile, the contenders had not awaited the court decision. For fourteen months, the Icelandic Coast Guard cut the trawl lines of British fishing boats, and on 29 October 1972, Icelanders fired blank shots across the bow of the British trawler *Real Madrid*. The West Germans experienced similar treatment. On 25 November 1972, the Icelandic Coast Guard vessel *Aegír* cut the trawl cables of the *Arcturus* and the *Erlangen*, and the loose end of a cut cable injured a German fisherman. On 28 December, the British *Brucella* collided with the Icelandic Coast Guard's *Odínn* in what the Coast Guard called "intentional ramming." A volcanic eruption in January brought a reprieve as Iceland needed its gunboats for rescue and salvage work, but twice in 1973, on 18 March and 26 May, Icelandic gunboats fired at British trawlers, the second time opening a hole.[12] In May 1973, the Heath government sent the Royal Navy to protect British fishing vessels. British trawlers wasted no time in returning to the disputed waters, accompanied by a weather ship, the *Miranda*, owned by the Department of Trade and Industry. Two other British ships, the *Ranger Briseis* (a converted factory trawler) and the *Othello*, provided medical and maintenance facilities which might no longer be available to British fishermen in Iceland. The ramming and cutting continued until the autumn of that year. In November 1973, London and Reykjavik finally reached a temporary agreement with Reykjavik In brief, it allowed British trawlers to fish in some parts of the disputed waters, but the British would limit their annual catch to 130,000 tons. There was no such agreement with the West Germans.[13]

Law of the Sea (LOS) talks, which had been taking place since 1958, were making very slow progress, and the government of Iceland had reason to think that direct action was necessary in order to preserve the fishery, which at best was finite. Indifference and complacency had led to the depletion of the cod stocks of the North Sea decades earlier.[14] In 1974, 137 nations attended a Law of the Sea Conference in Caracas, which reconvened in Geneva for eight weeks (17 March to 10 May) in 1975. There was progress in Caracas on the extension of territorial waters to twelve miles with limited sovereignty for another 188, a total of 200. What that would mean remained to be clarified at a session of the LOS conference scheduled for New York in March 1976.[15] Again, in July 1974, the International Court of Justice agreed with the British and the West Germans that the latest Icelandic extension was illegal.[16]

All four parties to the dispute had changes of leadership in 1974. In March, Harold Wilson replaced Edward Heath as British Prime Minister. In May, West

Germany had a spy scandal which forced the resignation of Willy Brandt, and Helmut Schmidt became the country's Chancellor. Gerald Ford replaced Richard Nixon 9 August, and on 28 August, Geir Hallgrímsson replaced Ólafur Jóhannesson. Icelanders had gone to the polls 30 June 1974, Hallgrímmsson's Independence Party gained three seats for a total of 25 of the 60 seats in the *Althing*, as compared with 22 after the election of 1971. The Communist People's Union managed to gain one seat for a total of 11.

The Ford Administration and Violence in the Anglo-Icelandic Dispute

The Ford administration had two interests to protect in Iceland: the U.S. Air Force and Navy base at Keflavik, and harmony among the NATO allies. It did not want to lose any NATO partner because of differences over the fishery.

The first issue (Keflavik) proved more readily soluble than the second (NATO harmony). Keflavik was significant for anti-submarine warfare. Both Soviet and U.S. authorities believed that the way to avoid war was to retain the capacity to inflict an intolerable level of damage on the other side if it dared to commit aggression. Land-based missiles were vulnerable to surprise attack, but submarines moved. NATO sensors in Norway and Denmark could detect any Soviet submarines in transit from the Baltic Sea to the Atlantic Ocean. From their base in Murmansk, Soviet submarines would pass between the United Kingdom and Iceland, and sensors at Keflavik helped to detect *them*.

At the same time, many Icelanders wondered whether a U.S. presence at Keflavik did or did not serve their interests. As early as 1948, Foreign Minister Bjarni Benediktsson noted that some of his compatriots feared that a U.S. military presence made Iceland a nuclear target.[17] On 15 December 1953, another Icelandic Foreign Minister—Kristinn Gudmundsson—complained that the presence of 5000 Americans, 80% of whom were military and 20% civilians—in a country whose total population was fewer than 150,000 necessarily had a significant impact.[18] Even if their behaviour had been universally exemplary, and of course it was not, Iceland had a limited supply of single women of marriageable age, and single Icelandic males could hardly have welcomed the competition. Moreover, U.S. military vehicles contributed to wear and tear on Icelandic roads.[19]

For the Ford administration, the election of a government led by Hallgrímsson and Hallgrímsson's selection of Einar Ágústsson as foreign minister meant a swift confirmation of the U.S. lease at Keflavik. Within a month of taking office, U.S. and Icelandic authorities agreed upon the terms of a new U.S. lease for the Keflavik base. A briefing paper prepared for President Ford before his first meeting with Prime Minister Hallgrímsson (at NATO headquarters, Brussels 30 May 1975) said:

> [Hallgrímsson's] advent was very welcome to the U.S., as his Independence Party had been active in working for the retention of our NATO base at Keflavik. Within one month of his assumption of office, the negotiations which had been going on with Iceland for nearly two years to determine the future of the status of the base were concluded on terms satisfactory to the U.S., Iceland and NATO. Hallgrimsson has been an especially good friend to the United States during a difficult period.[20]

Basically, the agreement provided that fewer Americans and more Icelanders would work at Keflavik and that the Americans would live on the base and keep a low profile.[21] Hallgrímsson and Ágústsson held office throughout Gerald Ford's presidency.[22] The bad news for the Ford administration was that during the campaign, the Independence Party had called for a 200-mile exclusive economic zone, to take effect 31 December 1975, after the current Anglo-Icelandic agreement expired. That proved to be a recipe for further violence.

The violence in the cod war was not one-sided, nor did it await December 1975. On 12 January 1975, at one of the regular meetings of the Secretary of State's Staff Meetings, the subject arose of violence which the British initiated. Assistant Secretary of State Joseph Sisco reported that twice the previous week, British vessels had rammed Icelandic ones. The government of Iceland then called for a NATO meeting to discuss the issue, and Sisco predicted that Iceland might sever diplomatic relations with the United Kingdom. The issue was "important" to the British, Sisco observed, but to Icelanders, it was a matter of "life-and-death."

Sisco saw that U.S. interests were at stake. Angry at the British/West German threat to the Icelandic economy and way of life, the government of Iceland might threaten to withdraw Iceland from NATO and to terminate the U.S. lease of the Keflavik base. Nor was there any easy solution. The British government demanded the right to take 110 thousand tons of fish per annum, while Reykjavik would agree only to 65,000. "You can split the difference or do something along those lines," said Sisco, but meanwhile, Icelandic protesters had already staged a temporary blockade of the Keflavik base. At that point, Kissinger expressed agreement that the U.S. had "become hostage to all of this." U.S. policy, said Sisco, was "to urge both sides to try to resolve this thing peacefully without our [U.S.] getting into the middle of it." In other words, U.S. policy was to hope that the British and Icelandic government could reach an agreement. Sisco noted with approval that NATO Secretary-General Joseph Luns was planning to visit Iceland. Sisco told the gathering that he had already informed British authorities that the dispute was far more vital to the Icelanders than to themselves, and he regretted that the British appeared utterly inflexible. Nobody at the meeting countered with a statement about the traditional U.S. position on open seas and highly restricted territorial limits or the need for the U.S. Navy to go anywhere, any time.[23]

Iceland, the Ford Administration, and the Law of the Sea

On 17 June 1975, Kissinger summarized U.S. policy on the Law of the Sea in a despatch to the United States Embassy in Moscow. John Morton Moore, said Kissinger, Chairman of the National Security Council Interagency Task Force on the Law of the Sea and Deputy Special Representative of the President for the Law of the Sea Conference, had outlined the U.S. position. Moore indicated that the Ford administration "was reviewing [the] entire question of unilateral fisheries legislation" and what to do about it. Under President Ford, wrote Kissinger, the United States government remained "opposed to any such legislation." The Ford administration's preference was a multilateral conference which would agree upon a Law of the Sea Treaty. Kissinger believed that this was also the Soviet position.[24]

Meanwhile, the dispute between Iceland and nations which claimed the right to fish within 200 miles of its coast remained unresolved. Late in June, Prime Minister Hallgrímsson went to London for talks, which appear to have been fruitless. On 15 July 1975, the government of Iceland said that it would enforce the extension of its exclusive fishing zone from 50 miles to 200. Iceland's Foreign Minister, Einar Ágústsson explained that the Anglo-Icelandic fishery agreement of 1973 was never intended to last beyond 13 November 1975, and he told the United Nations General Assembly that foreign fishermen, particularly those from the United Kingdom and West Germany, were depleting cod stocks to a dangerously slow level. The government of Iceland, said

Ágústsson, was willing to allow a limited number of British trawlers into waters between 50 and 200 miles from Iceland, but only on condition that the government of the United Kingdom actively promoted the sale of Icelandic fish to countries of the European Economic Community.[25]

On 15 August 1975, the U.S. Embassy in Reykjavik advised the Secretary of State that the government of Iceland intended to extend the territorial limit to 200 miles within two months. Iceland's Foreign Office admitted that "several other countries," including the United Kingdom and West Germany, had "formally sought negotiations," but the Icelandic government was only considering such requests. The Soviet Union had also protested the planned extension of Iceland's maritime borders. For its part, the United States Embassy advised the government of Iceland not to proceed too hastily. When the United States had extended its fisheries zone to 12 miles, said Ambassador Martin, it did not immediately exclude foreigners who had traditionally fished there. Canada acted in the same way under similar conditions, and when Brazil extended its fishery to 200 miles, it did too. According to the Ambassador, "Mexico, the USSR, and the UK have followed similar practices."[26]

On 30 September 1975, Foreign Minister Ágústsson had addressed the United Nations General Assembly and insisted on "a territorial sea of 12 miles [and] an exclusive economic zone of up to 200 miles."[27] Months later, the Hallgrímsson government unilaterally extended the maritime boundary to 200 miles, and resorted to violence.

Yet, there was progress. In the summer of 1975, President Ford travelled to the Finnish capital for a gathering of leaders of thirty-three of Europe's thirty-four countries (all except Albania) as well as himself and Canadian Prime Minister Pierre Elliott Trudeau. Arguably, the Helsinki Conference (the Conference on Security and Cooperation in Europe) would prove as significant as the last conference of its type, the Congress of Vienna, for the Helsinki accords proved decisive in ending the Cold War. The signatories agreed not to use force to change each other's existing boundaries and to permit certain basic human rights, which proved incompatible with the survival of the government of East Germany and perhaps other Communist governments. Notwithstanding the significance of the occasion, the Icelandic delegation focused on the fishery.[28] A State Department briefing paper for President Ford summarized the role of the Icelandic delegation, led by Prime Minister Hallgrímsson: "Iceland took a very low posture at CSCE, in keeping with its parochial (fisheries) focus of its foreign policy."[29]

Hallgrímsson must have made a strong impression when the two men met, for once President Ford returned to Washington, the White House recruited Eugene V. Rostow to mediate between Bonn and Reykjavik. When Ford had been a law student at Yale, Rostow had been one of his professors. Later Rostow served as an Assistant Secretary of State President during Lyndon Johnson's presidency.[30] With the Democrats' departure from the White House 20 January 1969, Rostow had returned to Yale University's School of Law, which granted him release time. Rostow's mediation was successful. Before the end of the calendar year, the Icelandic and West German governments managed to reach agreement. For the next two years, West Germany trawlers could fish within Iceland's 200 mile zone but would limit their annual catch to 60,000 tons. This was a genuine compromise. The Germans settled for less fish than what they had wanted, and the Icelanders agreed to a longer interim agreement than they desired. At the same time, there was no progress in the Anglo-Icelandic talks.[31]

Late in 1975 and early in 1976, the Anglo-Icelandic dispute again became violent. Talks between Prime Ministers Wilson and Hallgrímsson failed, and throughout January, British trawlers clashed with vessels of the Icelandic Coast guard. The Royal Navy went to the disputed waters, where Icelandic patrol boats were cutting the wires of British trawlers. On 28 December 1975, the British frigate *Andromeda* collided with the Icelandic vessel *Tyr*, and while Icelanders accused the *Andromeda* of deliberately ramming its target, the British issued denials. On 7 January, the *Andromeda* collided with the *Thor*, causing more serious damage. The frigate *Leander* collided with the *Thor* two days later, at which time both ships suffered damage. On 19 January, the Coast Guard's *Aegír* collided with a British trawler and opened a hole above the water line. That same day, Hallgrímsson threatened to sever diplomatic relations with the United Kingdom if it did not withdraw its frigates by 24 January, and Foreign Secretary British James Callaghan agreed to do so. However, Roy Hattersley, Minister of State at the Foreign and Commonwealth Office, said that they would return if Icelandic gunboats continued to harass British trawlers.[32]

The Anglo-Icelandic violence appeared on the agenda at the State Department Staff Meeting of 30 January 1976. By this time, the gap between the British and Icelandic positions had narrowed to 25,000 tons of fish, but passions were still running strongly. The British had reduced their demand to 85,000 tons of cod, while the Icelanders were offering 60,000. At the same time, said James Lowenstein, Deputy Assistant Secretary of State for European Affairs, the British were threatening to send their frigates back into the disputed waters within forty-eight hours, and the Icelanders were threatening new demonstrations and a withdrawal from NATO. Meanwhile, rumours were circulating throughout Iceland that some of the U.S. Navy ships at Keflavik were carrying nuclear weapons, and it was contrary to U.S. policy to issue confirmations or denials on such matters.

Participants at that meeting of 30 January 1976 discussed possible Icelandic withdrawal from NATO and an expiry of the lease on the Keflavik base. Sisco had been urging British authorities to make additional concessions and reminding the Icelanders that the British had already made a substantial retreat. Kissinger interjected:

> I think we better stop getting blackmailed by them [Icelandic authorities]. If they're going to use the base this way, they're going to close it anyway sometime—any time they're in a quarrel with some other country they threaten to close their base.
>
> I think the best contribution we can make is to tell them to go to hell—that if they want to close the base they can close it. The more nervousness we show, the more intransigent they're going to get. And I think we should stop running around after them.[33]

There were at least two other reasons why Kissinger could take the stand which he did. (1) The most obvious was that of power. Alone, either the United Kingdom or the Federal Republic of Germany was many times more powerful than Iceland could ever become. If Kissinger had to choose which of the three NATO allies was the most dispensable, it is hardly surprising that he chose Iceland. (2) American opinion was itself divided over the wisdom of the 200-mile exclusive fishing zone.

Many in Congress, controlled by Democrats, disagreed with the Republican administration of President Ford. They thought that the U.S. should do what others were doing and extend U.S. fishing rights to the 200 mile limit. Peru and other Latin American nations had extended their limits to 200 miles; the Trudeau government in Canada had declared its right to impose environmental controls to a distance of 100 miles; Greeks and Turks were confronting each other over Aegean waters claimed by both. Iceland's proclamation of a fifty-mile limit had actually led to shooting between Britons and Icelanders in the disputed waters, and a bilateral Anglo-Icelandic agreement of November 1973 settled the matter for only two years. Without an immediate unilateral claim to a 200-mile limit, thought many in New England's fishing industry, fishing boats from other countries—particularly Japan and the Soviet Union—would deplete the fish stocks off the U.S. coast while diplomats debated and discussed. The mayor of one Alaska community, C. Ross Wood of the Kodiak Island Borough, threatened that if the U.S. government would not protect the Alaska fishery, he would ask the Alaska State Government to proclaim a 200-mile exclusive fishing zone.[34] Kissinger suggested a series of bilateral agreements as interim measures as an alternative to the 200-mile limit.

On the other hand, Americans who fished for tuna off the coast of Ecuador opposed the 200-mile exclusive fishing zone as did the National Security Council (NSC). Proclamation and enforcement of a 200-mile exclusive fishing zone in the Bering Sea, warned the NSC, would produce a first class row with the Soviet Union and Japan. Other countries as well might decide that if the United States could unilaterally extend its limits, so could they. National Security Adviser Brent Scowcroft noted that besides Iceland, Costa Rica and Mexico had already extended their exclusive fishing zones to 200 miles, and a number of other coastal states—including Canada, Denmark, Kenya, Norway, Tanzania and the United Kingdom—were "under intense pressure to follow suit."[35] Secretary of State Kissinger advised President Ford to veto any unilateral extension approved by Congress. "Our ability to protect our distant-water fishermen from seizures when fishing in others' zones would be lessened," he warned. More ominously he added, "The prospect of resulting confrontations, particularly with the Soviet Union and Japan, would be a most serious matter with ramifications going beyond fisheries and the Law of the Sea."[36]

Days later, the violence resumed. Interference by the Coast Guard vessels *Baldur* and *Tyr* on 5 February prompted the British government to send the frigates *Juno* and *Diomede* back to the disputed waters that very day. Over the following two weeks, there were more collisions involving the *Tyr*, the *Juno*, the *Baldudr*, the *Thor*, the *Diomede*, and the *Aegír* Charges and counter-charges flew back and forth between Reykjavik and London, with accusations of jeopardy to life and at least one attempt to sink. Foreign Secretary Callaghan offered to allow observers from other NATO countries to board British frigates so that they could see for themselves what was happening, and Luns conveyed the message to the Icelandic government. The government of Iceland rejected the offer on the grounds that acceptance would imply the *legal right* of British vessels to be in the area, and on 19 February, Prime Minister Hallgrímsson announced that Iceland was severing diplomatic relations with the United Kingdom. The North Atlantic Council in Brussels expressed "deep regret," and Dr. Luns expressed his willingness to mediate. Satisfying as the rupture might have been to members of the *Althing*, who on 24 February gave the government of vote of confidence by a margin of 41:18, the collisions continued.[37]

In April 1976, Harold Wilson resigned and Callaghan became British Prime Minister. On 24 April 1976, Kissinger met Callaghan's successor as British Foreign Secretary, Anthony Crosland, and Crosland's permanent Under-Secretary, Sir Michael Palliser, at the Royal Air Force base at Waddington, Lincolnshire. Crossland and Palliser complained that the Icelanders were purchasing gunboats in the United States, and Kissinger lacked credible answers:

> *Crossland*: The Icelanders are shopping around for new and faster gun boats than what they have got now. The Icelanders are shopping around to buy, and your Government has wisely said there would be no lease from the [United States] Navy but they are free to shop around for boats on commercial terms. This has created an enormous uproar with my constituents over the idea of our boats' lines cut by U.S. boats. I don't know whether there are mothballed gunboats.

> *Kissinger*: There are two problems. Mothballed gunboats would be U.S. Navy, and we wouldn't do it. I don't see how they would be available on commercial terms.

Kissinger replied that Congress was considering a law that it must approve any commercial sale of military equipment worth $25 million or more. That did not satisfy Palliser, who responded: "You could probably get a lot of boats under that." Kissinger promised to "look into" the matter.[38]

Quietly, Kissinger supported the United Kingdom in this confrontation. During the confrontation, Washington not only rejected a request from the Hallgrímsson government to lease two fast patrol boats to Iceland but gave the British government advance notice of the rejection. Justice Minister Jóhannesson expressed "very deep disappointment" in Dr. Kissinger.[39]

Nevertheless, Anglo-Icelandic communication continued, albeit through intermediaries. During the diplomatic rupture, Norway assumed responsibility for protection of Icelandic interests in the United Kingdom, and France represented British interests in Iceland. Happily, both parties agreed to an interim solution signed in Oslo 1 June 1976. For its part, the British government agreed to limit the number of British trawlers in the disputed waters to no more than twenty-four per day. At no point would British vessels fish within twenty miles of the Icelandic coast, and in order to let the stocks reproduce, the British would refrain from fishing wherever and whenever Icelandic authorities instructed Icelandic fishermen to do so. In the face of criticism from those in engaged in Britain's fishing industry as well as Conservative Members of Parliament, Crosland described the interim agreement as the last which London would negotiate bilaterally with Reykjavik. Henceforth such agreements would be the responsibility of the entire European Economic Community. For his part, Ágústsson proclaimed victory. Iceland had the support of other Nordic governments (Denmark, the Faroes, Finland, Norway, and Sweden). The United Kingdom and Iceland resumed full diplomatic relations 2 June.

Epilogue and Conclusions

In conclusion, the Ford administration could claim success. It provided enough hope and pressure through such measures as the Rostow appointment and the cancellation of gunboat sales to encourage a settlement but did so in a sufficiently inoffensive way that all three parties to the Cod War—Iceland, West Germany, and the United Kingdom—remained in NATO. The U.S. even retained the Keflavik base. With benefit of hindsight, Icelanders could also be pleased. The Third United Nations Conference on the Law of the Sea continued throughout Jimmy Carter's presidency (20 January 1977-20 January 1981) and into that of Ronald Reagan.[40] In 1981, the tenth session concluded a draft treaty, and in 1982, delegates met again for a formal signing ceremony. The Convention, approved overwhelmingly, granted "every State...the right to establish the breadth of its territorial sea up to a limit of 12 nautical miles from coastal baselines" and an exclusive economic zone to a limit of 200 nautical miles.[41] Not surprisingly, Iceland was one of the Convention's supporters, as were Australia, Canada, the Scandinavian countries, and the Soviet bloc, including East Germany.[42] Icelanders, however, could be forgiven if they believed that David had defeated Goliath.

Notes

1. The author wishes to thank Geir Gundersen, archivist at the Gerald Ford Presidential Library; as well as Jan Drent and Bill Glover, for their helpful suggestions at the annual conference of the Canadian Nautical Research Society, held at Churchill, Manitoba, in August 2007.

2. For a review of the Ford administration's foreign relations challenges, see Graeme S. Mount, *895 Days that Changed the World: The Presidency of Gerald R. Ford* (Montreal: Black Rose Press, 2006).

3. Gerald R. Ford, *A Time to Heal: the Biography of Gerald R. Ford* (New York: Harper and Row, 1979); Henry Kissinger, *Years of Renewal* (New York: Simon and Schuster, 1999).

4. Douglas Brinkley, *Gerald R. Ford* (New York: Henry Holt and Company, 2007).

5. See, for example, letter of George S. Springsteen, State Department, to Brent Scowcroft, National Security Council, 24 Oct. 1975, PRESIDENTIAL NAME FILE, 1974-1977, Box 3, Folder: Rostow, Eugene V., Gerald Ford Presidential Library, Ann Arbor, Michigan. Cited hereafter as GFPL.

6. R.G. 59, General Records of the Department f State, Transcript of Secretary of State Henry Kissinger's Staff Meetings, Box 11, Folder: 12 October 1976, United States Archives, College Park, Maryland. Cited hereafter as Staff Meetings.

7. Major General John A. Wickam, Jr. Department of Defense, to National Security Adviser Brent Scowcroft, 19 Jan. 1976, National Security Adviser, PRESIDENTIAL COUNTRY FILES FOR EUROPE AND CANADA, Box 15, Folder: United Kingdom (6), GFPL.

8. Christine Ingebritsen, "Norm Entrepreneurs: Scandinavia's Role in World Politics," in Christine Ingebritsen, Iver Neumann, Sieglinde Gstöhl, and Jessica Beyer (editors), *Small States in International Relations* (Reykjavik: University of Iceland Press; Seattle: University of Washington Press, 2006), p. 284.

9. Ingebritsen, "Conclusions", in Ingebritsen et al, p. 289.

10. For background prior to 1972, see Mark Kurlansky, *Cod: A Biography of the Fish that Changed the World* (Toronto: Vintage Canada, 1998), pp. 144-163.

11. Edward Heath, *The Autobiography of Edward Heath: The Course of My Life* (London: Hodder and Stoughton, 1998), p. 701.

12. Kurlansky, p. 165.

13. For coverage of the 1971-1973 cod war, see *Keesing's Contemporary Archives*, 1973, pp. 25869-25876 and 26237-26239.

14. Kurlansky, pp. 144-145.

15. The Third United Nations Conference on the Law of the Sea, which began in 1970, continued with sessions in 1973, 1974, 1975, and 1976; see *Yearbook of the United Nations*, 1973, pp. 44-46; 1974, pp. 71-84, 1975, pp. 116-134; 1976, pp. 73-93.

16. *Keesing's Contemporary Archives*, 1976, p. 27511.

17. The Minister in Iceland (Richard Butrick), Reykjavik, to the Director of the Office of European Affairs (John D. Hickerson), 18 Aug. 1948, *Foreign Relations of the United States, 1948*, III, pp. 720-721. Cited hereafter as *FRUS*.

18. Memorandum of Conversation by the Assistant Secretary of State for European Affairs (Livingston Merchant), Paris, 15 December, 1953, *FRUS, 1952-1954*, VI, p. 1528.

19. Memorandum by the Director of the office of British Commonwealth and Northern European Affairs (G. Haydon Raynor) to the Assistant Secretary of State for European Affairs (Livingston Merchant), 25 Nov. 1953, *FRUS, 1952-1954*, VI, p. 1523.

20. National Security Adviser TRIP BRIEFING BOOKS AND CABLES FOR PRESIDENT FORD, 1974-1976, Box 8, Folder: May 28-June 3, 1975—Europe Briefing Book—NATO Bilaterals (4), GFPL.

21. National Security Adviser, NATIONAL SECURITY COUNCIL EUROPE, CANADA, AND OCEAN AFFAIRS, STAFF: FILES, Box 11, Folder: Iceland 1974 WH, GFPL.

22. Hallgrímsson and Ágústsson actually assumed office 28 August 1974, nineteen days after President Ford's inauguration. They remained in office until 1 September 1978.

23. Box 6, Folder: 12 January 1975, Staff Meetings, GFPL.

24. Secretary of State, Washington, to U.S. Embassy, Moscow, 17 June 1975, downloaded from CIA series CIA-RDP82S00697R0004000700001-8, National Archives of the United States, College Park, Maryland. Cited hereafter as CIA 1-8.

25. *Keesing's Contemporary Archives*, 1976, p. 27511.

26. U.S. Embassy, Reykjavik, to Secretary of State, Washington, 15 Aug. 1975, CIA-1-8.

27. *United Nations Monthly Chronicle*, XI, 9 (Oct. 1974), p. 92.

28. For a summary of the Ford administration and its role at Helsinki, see Mount, pp. 126-137.

29. Department of State Briefing Paper, National Security Adviser, Trip Briefing Books and Cables for President Ford, 1974-1976, Box 10, Folder: July 26-August 4, 1975—Europe Briefing Book, CSCE, GFPL.

30. The relationship at Yale between Ford and Rostow appears in Brinkley, p. 7.

31. "Denis Clift of the National Security Council" to National Security Adviser Brent Scowcroft, 26 Nov. 1975, National Security Adviser, PRESIDENTIAL NAME FILE, 1974-1977, Box 3, Folder: Rostow, Eugene V., GFPL.

32. *Keesing's Contemporary Archives*, 1976, pp. 27636-27638.

33. This and the following Sisco quotation come from Box 8, Folder: 30 January 1976, Staff Meetings, GFPL.

34. C. Ross Wood, Kodiak, to President Ford, Washington, 29 Oct. 1974, White House Central File: Subject File, Box 9, Folder: FO 3-1, International Waterways (1), GFPL.

35. For a summary of the arguments both in favour of and in opposition to a unilateral U.S extension of its exclusive fishing zone 200 miles from the nearest US-owned land, see the correspondence in White House Central Files Subject File, Box 10, Folder: FO 3-1/Fish-

eries, 10/18/75-11/30/75, and Folder: FO 3-1/Fisheries, 12/1/75-12/30/75, GFPL. The quotation and the reference to Ecuador come from a summary of a "Meeting with Congressional Opponents of 200-Mile Interim Fisheries Legislation, November 19, 1975" written by Scowcroft and filed in the second folder.

36. Kissinger to Ford, 6 April 1976, White House Central Files Subject File, Box 11, Folder FO 3-1, Fisheries, GFPL.

37. *Keesing's Contemporary Archives*, 1976, pp. 27637-27639.

38. Memorandum of Conversation, 24 April 1976, R.G. 59, Entry 5403 (Records of Henry Kissinger, 1973-77), Box 16, Folder: NODIS Memcoms April 1976, National Archives of the United States, College Park, Maryland.

39. *Keesing's Contemporary Archives*, 1976, pp. 27638, 27824-27825.

40. *Yearbook of the United Nations*, 1977, pp. 84-98; 1978, pp. 143-153; 1979, p. 120-131; 1980, pp. 136-159; 1981, pp. 126-140; 1982, pp. 178-247.

41. *Yearbook of the United Nations*, 1982, pp. 189 (the quotation) and 195.

42. *Yearbook of the United Nations*, 1982, pp. 241-242.

Chapter 4

Relations Between Trinidad and Tobago and the Neighbours

Despite the name, Trinidad and Tobago is one country. The name sounds plural, like that of the United States, but the two islands—Trinidad and Tobago—form one country with one government. Trinidad and Tobago deals as a unit with its neighbours and with the rest of the world.

On 18 April 1990, the President of Venezuela, Carlos Andrés Pérez, and the Prime Minister of Trinidad and Tobago, A.N.R. Robinson, signed a treaty, the Trinidad and Tobago-Venezuela Treaty on the Delimitation of Marine and Submarine Areas or Maritime Delimitation Treaty (MDT), which defined the maritime boundary between their two countries. The following year, Robinson's foreign minister, Sahadeo Basdeo, referred to the final ratification as "one of the finest moments in the history of relations between the two neighbouring republics."[1] There were precedents. In 1942, the United Kingdom and Venezuela concluded the Gulf of Paria Annexation Agreement. In 1985, the Trinidad and Tobago government of George Chambers (1981-1986) and the Venezuelan government of President Jaime Lusinchi (1984-1989) signed a fishing agreement. The following year, Chambers' foreign minister, Errol Mahabir, and representatives of both countries prepared a draft Maritime Boundary Delimitation Agreement.[2] In February 2004, when the Trinidad and Tobago government led by Patrick Manning was involved in a first class row with the Barbadian government of Owen Arthur over maritime boundaries and fishing rights, the MDT became a source of considerable controversy.

It may appear strange that the United Kingdom—the sovereign power in Trinidad and Tobago from 1797 until 1962—had not clarified the boundary with Spain, the sovereign power in the Viceroyalty of New Granada (modern Colombia, Ecuador, Panama, and Venezuela), nor with the successor state, Venezuela, which achieved independence in 1830. Pressure to do so had not been strong until 1942, when the British badly needed Venezuelan oil so that they could fight World War II. Then the United Kingdom and Venezuela *did* reach the Gulf of Paria Annexation Agreement, which the 1990 MDT subsequently abrogated and replaced.[3]

From the time that Trinidad and Tobago achieved independence in 1962, fishermen from Trinidad and Venezuela had had confrontations in the Gulf of Paria. Even the Venezuelan Coast Guard became involved. The government of George Chambers reached a provisional agreement with Venezuela in 1985, but it was good only for two years.[4] Subsequently, high level negotiations in both Caracas and Port of Spain in 1984 led to a series of temporary agreements on trade, the fishery, and a permanent maritime boundary between the two countries. In 1986, the last year during which the People's National Movement (PNM) under Chambers's leadership held office, Venezuela concluded a fisheries agreement with Trinidad and Tobago, and the two parties prepared a draft Maritime Boundary Delimitation Agreement. Then, in December 1986, parliamentary elections in Trinidad and Tobago saw the defeat of the PNM and the formation of a new government led by A.N.R. Robinson, leader of the National Alliance for Reconstruction (NAR). Robinson's foreign minister, Sahadeo Basdeo and his Venezuelan counterpart, signed the MDT in 1990, and both countries approved the agreement shortly thereafter.

The parliamentary opposition, led by future Prime Minister Patrick Manning, Chambers' successor as leader of the People's National Movement (PNM), was highly critical. Manning charged that the NAR was making too many concessions to Venezuela. The NAR government, said Manning, was not aware of the value of the fishery and the mineral rights beneath the waters which it was ceding to Venezuela, and Manning estimated that Venezuela was gaining an area equivalent to the size of Trinidad itself. Another problem with the MDT, thought Manning, was that it failed to take into account the claims and interests of Barbados and Guyana, like Trinidad and Tobago members of both the Commonwealth and Caricom (Caribbean Community).[5]

Robinson's Foreign Minister, Sahadeo Basdeo, challenged Manning and defended the treaty. Unlike Manning, whose job was to criticize, Basdeo held the responsibility which accompanied high office. Basdeo replied that the Government of Trinidad and Tobago "would always be receptive to consultations with the Governments of neighbouring coastal states that might consider themselves prejudiced by the Delimitation Treaty line."[6] Of course, this did not commit anyone to very much. Talk is cheap, and "consultation" falls short of "agreement." With regard to Barbados, Basdeo noted that the United Nations Conference on the Law of the Sea (UNCLOS) allowed a sovereign nation to claim an Exclusive Economic Zone (EEZ) to a maximum of 200 nautical miles from its shores. However, he noted, Tobago was a mere 119 nautical miles from Barbados. This meant that the rules of UNCLOS were inadequate in this case. Barbados would have to conclude some bilateral agreement with Trinidad and Tobago before either would know the extent of its EEZ.[7] Prime Minister Robinson said in February 1990 that he had not instructed his foreign minister to negotiate with Barbados. The problem at the time was the maritime boundary between Trinidad and Tobago and Venezuela, and negotiations took place between those two countries alone.[8] In agreement that the 1990 treaty was irrelevant to the dispute of 2004 was Professor Julian Kenny, a Trinidadian authority on the Law of the Sea.[9]

(Significantly, in February 2004 Prime Minister Manning's Foreign Minister, Knowlson Gift, would defend the 1990 Trinidad and Tobago-Venezuela Treaty on the Delimitation of Marine and Submarine Areas. Not only would there be international chaos, he said, if governments were to repudiate legally registered boundary agreements. The 1990 treaty did not affect the rights of Guyana, as witnessed by Guyanese silence on the matter, and it provided the kind of international stability which investors would like.[10])

The very day—Monday, 16 February 2004—when Arthur called for binding arbitration from the United Nations, there was also some good news. According to the *Daily Express*, "The list of affected [Trinidad and Tobago] products—including fruit and vegetables, beer, aerated beverages, fish and ice cream—was to have been gazetted and made public yesterday. But it did not happen.[11]

Nevertheless, Trinidad and Tobago prepared for the worst. On 28 March 2004, *Sunday Newsday* carried the headline: "TT appoints top British QC to tribunal on maritime boundary dispute with Barbados" The story said that the Manning government had designated "a leading Queen's Counsel in public international law as a member of the arbitral tribunal on the pending arbitration between TT and Barbados, one Professor Ian Brownlie. from the United Kingdom, renowned as "the dean" of public international law. The Trinidadian newspaper *Sunday Newsday* said that Professor Brownlie would serve as a member of the tribunal "to be constituted to settle the issue of the Delimitation of the Exclusive Economic Zone and Continental Shelf between Trinidad and Tobago and Barbados." The government of Trinidad and Tobago, said *Sunday Newsday*, had also designated Attorney General John Jeremie and , like Brownlie, another resident of the United Kingdom, John Almeida, as advisors in connection with the forthcoming arbitration. The two governments—those of Trinidad and Tobago as well as that of Barbados—would attempt to find three other arbitrators, but if they could not agree on the appointments, United Nations Secretary General Kofi Annan would prepare a short-list and the President of the International Tribunal for the Law of the Sea would decide who would serve. If Owen Arthur wanted to proceed through the United Nations, the Manning government indicated, Trinidad and Tobago was prepared.[12]

While Barbados was arguing with Trinidad and Tobago, Guyana revealed that in 2002, the Government of Guyana "had filed an official protest with the United Nations" against the 1990 MDL. At the same time, it had protested to the governments of Venezuela and of Trinidad and Tobago. Guyana's High Consul to Trinidad and Tobago, Ernie Ross, made the announcement 18 February. During a telephone interview with the *Trinidad Guardian*, Ross declared that Guyana should participate in any talks about Barbados' objections to the MDL. The United Nations and not Caricom should deal with the issue, said Ross.[13]

Despite the Maritime Delimitation Treaty, there still were some confrontations in the Gulf of Paria. In April 1993, shots rang out as fishing boats from Trinidad and Tobago went to waters which Trinidad and Tobago Foreign Minister Ralph Maraj had described as "out of bounds." In February 1994, the Coast Guard of Trinidad and Tobago stormed a Venezuelan fishing trawler which had defied orders to stop and instead attempted to ram the Coast Guard vessel.[14] In

1996, there were new reports that the Venezuelan Navy had shot at fishermen from Trinidad and Tobago.[15] On 16 February 2004, one McDonald James of Couva noted in a letter to the editor of the *Trinidad Guardian* that "Venezuelans...routinely jail and fish greedy Trinidad fishermen who raid their shrimp breeding ground." Valid as James's argument was, there might also be other explanations. Buoys placed in the Gulf of Paria at the time of the 1990 agreement to mark the border had disappeared with the passage of time, and it was possible that some crews might not have known in whose waters they actually were. Also, as few Trinidadian fishermen were fluent in Spanish and most Venezuelans could not speak English, there certainly were possibilities for misunderstanding.

Illegal activities by Trinidadians would prove lethal during the next few weeks, when the Venezuelan Coast Guard clearly had higher priorities than patrols of the Gulf of Paria. On 20 March 2004, pirates from Venezuela boarded a Trinidadian fishing boat one mile from the Venezuelan coast. The three Trinidadians aboard the vessel had to jump overboard, and the oldest one, Rupert Bissoon, 55, gave his life jacket so that the other two, Deodath Bissoon, 17, and Denver Beharry, 28, might stand some chance of survival. Rupert drowned, and the other two spent seven hours in the water before being rescued. The Trinidadian newspaper *Newsday* reported that the Coast Guard has been asked to patrol so that fishermen from Cedros and Icacos will have some protection. The three came from Icacos, and Deodath was a student at Cedros Composite School.[16]

Another Trinidadian newspaper, *The Daily Express* (p. 10) carried an angry editorial about the weekend's pirates. Under the title "Track down pirates, murderers," the editorial said:

> Given by the pirates the alternative of either being shot on the spot or walking the plank, as it were, the three fishermen chose the only way out, which was to jump into the sea.
>
> Only after the three jumped did the pirates toss a lifejacket...
>
> [All fishermen] will be reluctant...[to] ply the threatened waters...
>
> We urge our Government to protest in the strongest terms to its Venezuelan counterpart. It is not that we do not know that these pirates are a law unto themselves. However, given President Hugo Chavez's warm and reciprocal embrace of his nearest Caribbean neighbour, we expect

that the authorities will do all in their power to investigate this incident, track down these murderers, and bring them to face the justice they deserve. It is the least we can do for one lost Trinidadian.[17]

Another death would follow. On 28 March 2004, reporter Susan Boodram-Mohanmmed of *Sunday Newsday* reported that Friday at 11 a.m., Venezuelan pirates murdered Shane Abraham of Bonasse Village, age 21, and robbed, beat, and ambushed his two fellow crew members. "The government can't expect a poor fisherman to protect himself when we are dealing with bandits with guns and other weapons. We are feeding the country, so the government should take care of us," Cedros fisherman Feraz Ali told *Sunday Newsday*. Ali is the owner of the fishing vessel in which Abraham had been employed for the last five months. Cedros, a prosperous community with many fine homes, was largely Muslim.

A story by Neidi Lee-Sing Rojas added more details. One fisherman said, "Our only hope is to walk on water like Jesus Christ, or die.

The Coast Guard have said they cannot help the fishermen once they are in Venezuelan waters. "We have to take a chance. There is nothing for us to catch in our waters so we have to go further out," said one man, known as "Sharkhead." ...

Venezuelan Ambassador to TT, Hector Azocar, said he was concerned about the increasing number of piracy attacks against fishermen in this country and has agreed to meet with the relevant authorities to try and work out the problems.

Azocar was speaking with *Sunday Newsday* last week when he noted that while some fishermen were innocently attacked, there were others who engaged in illegal activities. "So the situation is very complicated, but this is one problem we have to address," he said.

Azocar noted that Venezuela and Trinidad and Tobago did have a disclosed that there was currently a bilateral Commission to deal with such measures but agreed that it had long been dormant. The Ambassador said that his government was definitely open to discussions. He also said "he was also aware that a number of the piracy incidents against TT fishermen have not been reported to the Venezuelan authorities and indicated there was a need to have more co-operation between the TT and Venezuelan Coast Guard[s]."[18]

On 31 March, *The Trinidad Guardian* editorialized that in any bilateral talks with Venezuela, Trinidad and Tobago would be negotiating from a position of weakness. The Trinidad and Tobago Coast Guard was ill-equipped to protect fishermen from pirates in the Gulf of Paria, it said:

> WHEN Cedros fishermen complained to the media on Sunday that the Coast Guard patrol in the area had only one pirogue, many readers must have assumed that was a bitter joke...
>
> On Monday, Lt Commander Mark Williams of the T&T Coast Guard admitted that the fishermen's claim was true: there is indeed only one pirogue attached to the Coast Guard base at Cedros.
>
> Lt Cmdr Williams added that in addition, other Coast Guard boats patrol the area.
>
> One would hope so, because the idea that fishermen in those waters could be protected or assisted in any way by a single pirogue would be laughable if it were not a matter of life and death.
>
> And the Coast Guard's watch over that area is not only a matter of guarding fishermen.
>
> Some years ago, the U.S. assisted in setting up and equipping the Coast Guard base in Cedros not for the sake of fishermen but because the easy access to Venezuela from that part of Trinidad makes it a choice location for trans-shipping cocaine and other contraband goods. That fact has not changed; neither has the need for constant vigilance by the security forces.
>
> But if other Coast Guard vessels do in fact patrol in those waters, they have escaped the notice of local fishermen, suggesting that their patrols are exceedingly stealthy—and if they are not noticed by local fishermen, can they hope to act as a deterrent to pirates? Or perhaps the patrols are very rare, in which case, again, they cannot hope to be effective.
>
> Lt Cmdr Williams' bold assertion that "We are taking all steps necessary to avert sea piracy" was meant to reassure. But how could it, when in the past two weeks alone two fishermen have died at the hands of pirates and two others were lucky to escape alive?...

On 2 April, *The Trinidad Guardian's* editorial cartoon showed a Coast Guard officer sleeping in a hammock while people in a boat yelled "Pirate! Help! Help!"

Nor was *The Trinidad Guardian* alone in its thinking. A telephone poll on Channel 6 news 1 April 2004 indicated that 70% of those who called thought that the Coast Guard could be more effective. An Opposition politician, Gilliam Lucky, MP, blamed the government for neglecting the Coast Guard.[19]

On 3 April, *Saturday Newsday* reported that residents of Cedros were still angry that members of the governng PNM cabinet had not really met with them to discuss protection from piracy in the Gulf of Paria. Nor was it helpful that the Member of Parliament for Cedros, Larry Achong, had recently resigned as Minister of Labour in order to protest government policy toward the natural gas workers at Point Fortin. Achong sided with his striking constituents, who wanted higher wages, rather than with his cabinet colleagues. April 3's *Trinidad Guardian* editorialized under the caption, "Ministers' Cedros mission insensitive":

> The mission involved a dramatic touchdown on the Cedros Savannah of a National Security helicopter, bringing to the troubled village two high-level Cabinet Ministers and the highest Army and Coast Guard officers...

> The arrival of Mr. Joseph and Foreign Minister Knowlson Gift raised villagers' expectations...

> They were disappointed. The Ministers and the military top brass stepped from the helicopter, climbed into a jeep with tinted windows, shut themselves into a room at the Cedros Security Complex, and refused to meet any but a handful of the assembled villagers, including the embarrassed Mr. Achong...

> For fisherfolk nightly under the gun in the Gulf, this was not just insensitive. It was a straightforward putdown—a declaration that a life-and-death matter for poor fisherfolk was somehow too "high" for a Minister to discuss with them...

That same day, 3 April 2004, *Saturday Newsday* carried a statement from National Security Minister Martin Joseph that the PNM government had "been doing intelligence work on incidents of piracy off Trinidad's South West coast, which resulted in the deaths of two fishermen." The *Trinidad Guardian* also reported action. Chief of Defence Staff Ancil Antoine, said reporter Yvonne Webb, had told a press conference held in Cedros following a "closed-door" meeting between cabinet ministers and fishermen that the government was about to implement a plan which involved the use of "radar, aircraft, vessel and surveillance on land..." in order to protect Trinidad and Tobago, "by sea, land and air... [against] arms and illicit drugs." Residents of Cedros had wanted to discuss "piracy" and the two recent deaths. At that meeting, National Security Minister Joseph said that he would consider issuing flare guns to fishermen to use in case of distress. A boat captain named Sirju Singh, skipper of the boat on which Shane Abraham had died, made the suggestion even though he had been denied admission to the meeting, and Joseph later deemed the idea as "excellent."[20]

Pressure on the government of Trinidad and Tobago continued, but although thanks to oil that country is one of the Caribbean's most prosperous nations, there are limits to what a country with a population of roughly one million people can afford. *Newsday*'s edition of 6 April 2004 carries a story entitled "Border security remains top priority." According to *Newsday*, National Security Minister Joseph had said as much and said that the government planned "to acquire two state-of-the art naval vessels for the Coast Guard and to strengthen Trinidad and Tobago's existing coastal radar network."

Joseph further explained:

He said acquisition of two Offshore Patrol Vessels (OPVs) for the Coast Guard and strengthening of the coastal radar system were very much on the front burner but declined to give details because it was not "in national security's interest."

"All I can tell you is that work is afoot as it relates to ensuring that the technical competence that we need to have in order to enhance performance of our protective services—that's afoot." The OPVs each have the capacity to carry a helicopter (with offensive/research-rescue capabilities), two fast interceptors and an amphibious assault team of 150 soldiers.

Cabinet approval for the OPVs was given in September 2003. The National Security Minister, Howard Chin Lee, said in Parliament on October 10, 2003, that the Coast Guard would be receiving six interceptor vessels at a cost of $2 million, while the Coast Guard's Staubles Bay base was being upgraded to accommodate the OPVs, the TTS Nelson and the CG Six.

Chin Lee also indicated that the coastal radar surveillance system would become operational within six months, allowing "total coverage of our coastal waters."

Chin Lee said funds from a U.S.$ 945,000 agreement with the United States government would be used to develop the system which would be similar to one currently being used by the Israeli military.

He said when the PNM assumed office in December 2001, only three percent of TT's coastal waters were under radar surveillance.

While residents of Cedros pressured the Manning government and the Manning government reflected on that pressure, illegal activity continued in the Gulf of Paria. Events of Good Friday, perhaps chosen on the assumption that law enforcement authorities would not be at work, were particularly shocking. On 11 April, Easter Sunday, *Newsday* carried a story written by Robin Morais about smuggling from Venezuela—"Fishermen held with smuggled birds":

TWO FISHERMEN were arrested on Good Friday morning with 30 birds believed to have been smuggled from neighbouring Venezuela.

They were held in a joint sting exercise involving Customs and Excise officers and a Coast Guard officer who were on patrol off the waters of Chacachacare.

An informed source also told *Newsday* [that] the birds were bull finches and that all of them were already dead.

The source added that the bull finches were drowned by the smugglers who threw them into the sea while they were still caged.

"They were trying to get rid of their illegal cargo by trying to dump it when they saw the customs vessel approaching them," the source said.

The source revealed that the birds were being smuggled into TT from Venezuela and taken to Staubles Bay, where they [the smugglers?] were charged by Customs and Excise Division officers.

Game Wardens and police were also present at Staubles Bay to identify the species of birds.

The source disclosed that the smugglers were charged with the illegal importation of restricted/prohibited goods and are due to appear before the Comptroller of Customs or one of his representatives on Tuesday morning.

Furthermore, the source revealed that the two persons needed a licence from the Forestry Division to import the birds in[to] TT. He said the smugglers were not armed when they were arrested by members of the Customs Marine Interdiction Unit.

The source said that the smugglers' boat, a pirogue, was detained by the customs officers pending the outcome of the matter.

He said that there had been an increase over the last year in the illegal smuggling of endangered birds and wildlife like monkeys from the Venezuelan mainland to TT.

The source said the smugglers had been using the waters off TT's western peninsula as their rendezvous point on the wildlife smuggling routes, hence the Customs Marine Interdiction Unit increasing their patrols to counteract such illegal activities.

By 2004, the Venezuela-Trinidad and Tobago Maritime Delimitation Treaty had become highly controversial for yet another reason. This time, the problem was not Venezuela but Barbados, which calls itself "the land of the flying fish." As long as both Barbados and Trinidad and Tobago were British colonies, a boundary seemed unnecessary. There were plenty of fish in the sea, and residents of one part of the British Empire were free to move to other parts. Even after independence (Trinidad and Tobago in 1962, Barbados in 1966), decades passed before action seemed imperative. Eventually all parties realized that the number of flying fish was finite. In November 1990, representatives from Barbados and Trinidad and Tobago had met in Trinidad and signed an agreement which regulated the fishery throughout calendar year1991. Marine biologists advised both parties on the spawning and migratory habits of the flying fish, and, acting in good faith, officials arranged what at the time seemed a sensible accord. During spawning season, there would be no fishing at all. Spawning season lasted for three months. Thereafter, when the fish swam into Barbadian waters, Barbadians could catch them. When they swam into the territorial waters of Trinidad and Tobago off the coast of Tobago, citizens of the Trinidad and Tobago could catch them. There were no limits on the quantities which might be taken. Talks to extend, modify, or replace the accord should begin no later than 1 October 1991.[21]

Before the 1990 accord between Barbados and Trinidad and Tobago expired, the NAR government of Trinidad and Tobago suffered defeat at the polls, and the PNM returned to office. As far as it was concerned, a fishing agreement with Barbados was not a high priority. As there seemed to be enough flying fish for everyone's requirements, no negotiations took place either to extend the 1990 agreement nor to modify it.

The PNM was not the only party at fault in this matter. From 1995 until 2001, the United National Congress (UNC) formed the government of Trinidad and Tobago, and it too ignored the issue. Studying the travels and the sex life of flying fish was not the most exciting activity for diplomats. Even so, in December 2001 the Coast Guard of Trinidad and Tobago seized Barbadians who were fishing and held them for a short time.[22]

Early in 2003, by which time the PNM had returned to office, still under the leadership of Patrick Manning, it was clear that there was a flying fish problem. On 22 January, Barbadian Prime Minister Owen Arthur wrote to Manning with the suggestion that it was time to consider another agreement on flying fish. Months passed in which little happened. In December, heads of Commonwealth governments met in Nigeria, and after the conference Manning said that he and Arthur had discussed the issue there. Arthur issued a public denial.[23] In the first half of February 2004, the Coast Guard of Trinidad and Tobago "intercepted and detained" two Barbadian fishermen, Joseph Mason, 47, and Samuel Firebrace, 61, for poaching off the coast of Trinidad and Tobago in what clearly were the territorial waters of the twin island republic.[24] Despite their quick release, the government of Barbados threatened such reprisals as prohibitive duties on imports from Trinidad and Tobago and protection from the Barbadian Coast Guard for Barbadian fishing vessels which might enter disputed waters.[25] Even landlubbers became involved. When musicians from Trinidad and Tobago performed at a concert in Barbados, the audience of 30,000 cheered lustily when Barbadians were centre stage but sat in silence or booed the visitors.[26] A Trinidadian audience sat in silence or heckled "Go fry some flying fish" when Barbadian superstar "Timmy" sang in Port of Spain. A *Barbados Nation* journalist who had covered Trinidad's Carnival "for years" refused to do so in 2004, and other Barbadians called for a boycott of the event.[27] The situation was serious. Would the tariffs on goods from Trinidad and Tobago violate the Caricom Treaty and perhaps jeopardize Caricom itself? Might the Coast Guard of Trinidad and Tobago shoot at the Barbadian Coast Guard?[28]

There were two issues at stake. The first concerned the fish. How many constituted a reasonable catch? In whose waters they were caught was less important, for if too many disappeared too quickly, the stocks would diminish no matter where the action happened. The second was a maritime boundary agreement between Barbados and Trinidad and Tobago.[29] Prime Minister Manning realized that a boundary for fish might establish a precedent for a boundary affecting ownership of oil, natural gas, and other mineral rights on the underwater continental shelf. Manning also complained that his hands were tied. The 1990 Venezuela-Trinidad and Tobago Maritime Delimitation Treaty, he said, had ignored the rights of Barbados and Guyana. Unfortunately, what the NAR government had conceded despite his objections in 1990 and registered at the United Nations was lost forever. Trinidad and Tobago could not repudiate the 1990 treaty without creating problems with Venezuela and perhaps other Latin American countries. Yet, as long as the 1990 treaty remained in effect, Trinidad and Tobago could not satisfy the legitimate claims of Barbados and, should they arise, Guyana.[30]

On 16 February, Arthur took decisive action. After a luncheon in a posh Barbadian hotel with Manning, Arthur issued a statement. (There was no joint communiqué.) As far as his country was concerned, said Arthur, the MDT was irrelevant, and he was taking the issue to the United Nations. Arthur said:

> [T]he Venezuela/Trinidad and Tobago Treaty of 1990 is not binding or relevant to Barbados or any other third state. It purports unilaterally to appropriate to Venezuela and Trinidad and Tobago an enormous part of Barbados' and Guyana's maritime territory, as well as one-third of Guyana's land territory.
>
> As Prime Minister of Barbados, I cannot be complicit in any agreement which threatens to usurp territory, maritime or land, that is contrary to international law, let alone the national interest of any Caricom state, including Barbados. In fact, all members of the Conference Heads of Government of Caricom annually reaffirm their commitment to support the territorial integrity with respect to the Venezuelan claim.
>
> I believe that Prime Minister Manning shares my assessment that there is no possibility of a negotiated settlement of the maritime boundary between Barbados and Trinidad and Tobago that does not compromise the interests of Barbados and Guyana. Those interests are confirmed

and have their legal justification in the United Nations Convention on the Law of the Sea (UNCLOS), of which Barbados, Guyana, and Trinidad and Tobago are all parties.[31]

In 2004, the government of Barbados asked the United Nations for an interpretation of the Law of the Sea. On 11 April 2006, the decision by the International Court in The Hague was so ambivalent that both countries claimed victory. In the short run, no one was humiliated, but ambiguity is hardly a key to a long-term solution. As for Venezuela, whose population is twenty-six times that of Trinidad and Tobago and whose capacity for arms and surveillance purchases is at least twenty-six times stronger, there is no way in which Trinidad and Tobago can compete. Good will between the two neighbours serves the interests of both countries, and certainly that of the smaller of the two. The availability of GPS equipment probably renders a line of buoys through the Gulf of Paria less necessary than it was in 1990, but divided jurisdictions are often tempting to lawbreakers. They can perform their actions on one side of the border, then take refuge on the other. Fishermen willing to fish in another country's waters, smugglers of exotic animals, and drug traffickers are willing to take risks. Sometimes they are unsuccessful and pay a high price. On other occasions, they succeed and enjoy the fruits of their illegal labour. The maritime boundaries of Trinidad and Tobago provide an ongoing challenge to whichever governments hold office in Port of Spain, the national capital, and are likely to do so for the foreseeable future.

Notes

1. Sahadeo Basdeo and Graeme Mount, *The Foreign Relations of Trinidad and Tobago, 1962-1990* (Port of Spain: Lexicon, 2001), p. 142.

2. Basdeo and Mount, p. 64.

3. Rita Taitt, "How the 'flying fish war' came to be", *Sunday Newsday*, 15 Feb. 2004. Cited hereafter as Taitt.

4. The Centre for International Relations, located on the campus of the University of the West Indies in St. Augustine, Trinidad, has a series of ten microfiches with clippings of fishing disputes between Trinidadians and Venezuelans.

5. Taitt.

6. Taitt.

7. Taitt.

8. Ria Taitt, "Robinson surprised Treaty now a source of tension", *Newsday*, 18 Feb. 2004.

9. Channel 6 News, 7 p.m., Port of Spain 17 Feb. 2004.

10. Address of Knowlson Gift "to the nation", delivered 20 February 2004, and printed in the *Trinidad Guardian* 21 February 2004.

11. *Daily Express*, 17 Feb. 2004.

12. *Sunday Newsday*, 28 March 2004.

13. *Trinidad Guardian*, 19 Feb. 2004.

14. Basdeo and Mount, p. 201.

15. *Daily Express*, 31 Oct. 1996; *Trinidad Guardian*, 31 Oct. 1996.

16. *Newsday*, 22 March 2004.

17. *Daily Express*, 23 March 2004.

18. *Sunday Newsday*, 28 March 2004.

19. An op-ed column by Lucky, *Trinidad Guardian*, 2 April 2004.

20. The meeting took place 1 April 2004 and Webb's report appeared in *The Trinidad Guardian* 3 April.

21. Interview with Brinsley Samaroo, Minister of Agriculture in the NAR government and chief negotiator for Trinidad and Tobago in the 1990 talks with Barbados, Mayaro, Trinidad, 14 Feb. 2004; also Marisa Camejo, "Taking (Fish) Stock in Trinidad and Tobago Waters", *Sunday Express*, 15 Feb. 2004. Cited hereafter as Camejo.

22. Column of Rickey Singh, *Saturday Express*, 14 Feb. 2004.

23. Camejo; also front page of *Daily Express*, 4 Feb. 2004.

24. *Sunday Express*, 8 Feb. 2004. See also the article by Darren Bahaw in the 4 April 2004 edition of *The Sunday Express*.

25. Donna Yawching's column, *Sunday Newsday*, 15 Feb. 2004. Cited hereafter as Yawching.

26. Rory Rostant, "Bajan crowd takes side in fishing dispute as Machel given cold reception", *Sunday Newsday*, 15 Feb. 2004.

27. Kenroy Ambis, "Cold shoulder for Bajan Act", *Daily Express*, 17 Feb. 2004.

28. Yawching.

29. Julian Kenny wrote a lengthy essay on the legal implications of the dispute between Barbados and Trinidad and Tobago, which appeared on the op-ed page (p. 11) of the *Daily Express*, 10 Feb. 2004. See also the editorial in the *Daily Express*, 5 Feb. 2004.

30. Taitt; also Trinidad and Tobago Television News, 12 Feb. 2004; *Daily Express*, 13 Feb. 2004.

31. Statement of Barbadian Prime Minister Owen Arthur, reprinted in *Daily Express*, 17 Feb. 2004.

SECTION II
ENFORCING BORDERS

Chapter 5

The Borders of the Former Yugoslavia and of Romania

Since World War I (except during World War II), historians around the globe have met every year divisible by five. For reasons of economy and language, most university professors who teach history normally study either their own country or *one* other. The goals of the International Congress on Historical Sciences are to allow historians from one country to exchange ideas and information with historians of others and thereby to promote international understanding. The 1980 gathering took place in Romania, then under the heel of the notorious dictator Nicolae Ceauşescu, who wanted to promote the idea that Romania had a 2050-year-old claim on Transylvania. Transylvania had been Hungarian territory until the 1919 Treaty of Trianon, and the irridentist spirit in Hungary was far from dead.[1]

Several months before the Bucharest conference, a friend who taught in Laurentian University's Geography Department, Joe Konarek, suggested that we—and our wives—might rent a car and tour Yugoslavia before the conference. Joe was Czech by birth and had some familiarity with Slavic languages, including Croatian. Croatian and Serb are mutually intelligible. Joan (my wife) and I jumped at the opportunity, and another friend, Gwynneth Hughes, joined Joe, his wife Barbara, Joan and me. On 26 July 1980, we flew from Canada to Dubrovnik on the Dalmatian coast, then drove inland to Sarajevo, and south to what is now The Republic of Macedonia. There we divided our time between its capital, Skopje, and Ohrid (pronounced OWE-chrid), located on a lake of the same name.

Yugoslavia perennial leader, Josip Broz Tito, had died earlier in the year, but Yugoslavia had not yet begun to disintegrate, at least visibly. The situation appeared calm, and good will was ubiquitous. Air pollution and the quality of the highways left much to be desired, but there was no shortage of good food, and we tourists could fraternize with Yugoslavs. Many Yugoslavs rented rooms in their homes to foreigners at the height of the tourist season, and the five of us stayed in one such bed-and-breakfast at Ohrid over the weekend corresponding to Canada's Civic Holiday Weekend, Simcoe Day Weekend in Ontario.

Ohrid was but a short distance from the Albanian border, the other side of which was out of bounds to travellers from Ohrid. This was the era of Enver Hoxha (pronounced HO-ja), Albanian dictator from 20 November 1944 until 11 April 1985. Although never officially Head of State or President, Hoxha was unquestionably the leader, and Albanians—citizens of Europe's poorest country —had less personal freedom than anyone else on that continent. Hoxha's Albania was a closed country, off limits to most foreigners; for their part, few Albanians had the legal right ever to leave Albania. Lake Ohrid was partly in Yugoslavia, partly in Albania, the way Lake Champlain, Lake of the Woods, and four of the Great Lakes are partly in Canada and partly in the United States.

Sunday afternoon we drove south from Ohrid to the border at Sveti Naum. Two landmarks dominated the border area: an Orthodox monastery and a magnificent beach. Perhaps the people who determined the border's location had placed it in such a way that the monastery would be inside Macedonia. Metres from the border, hundreds of picnickers on the beach ate, danced, and chatted. The lake had a sandy bottom, and the water was delightfully warm for swimming. Apart from a watchtower at a high elevation in the distance, we could see no signs of life on the Albanian side of the border, and on our side, there was no tension. Residents of the area had become used to the idea that there was a crazy guy next door, and they did not expect Hoxha to do anything to *them*. The sole indication that the situation was in any way bizarre was a patrolling Yugoslav police boat which could warn swimmers and boaters not to go one bay too far to the south.

From Ohrid, we drove to Belgrade, where Friday evening we boarded the train to Bucharest. As it was an overnight train, the five of us had thought of purchasing sleeping accommodation, and Joe and I actually went to the appropriate office to make the purchase. The counter had the shape of a capital "L," with the longer side selling tickets on trains within Yugoslavia, the shorter on international trains. Huge signs advertised the joys of train rides to Hanoi and Pyongyang. A huge staff came, went, and chatted behind the international counter, but in the hour or two we were there we did not witness a single clerk serving a single customer. Finally I said to Joe, "Rather than spend the rest of the day here, I would prefer to see as much of Belgrade as possible even if we have to sit up all night." It was a wise choice.

Darkness had fallen before the train left Belgrade, and the train was a Romanian one. This was both good and bad. It was good because the signs were in Romanian, which all of us could read. The Romanian language is an offshoot of Latin, like French or Italian, and closer to the original than any Romance language other than Spanish. Romanian uses the Latin alphabet, not the Cyrillic. The five of us came from the generation educated when authorities believed that anyone worthy of a university education ought to be sufficiently talented and self-disciplined to learn Latin, and we had studied it. The bad news was the state of the washrooms. They lacked a single drop of water, and the toilets looked as though they had never been flushed since Ceauşescu had come to power in 1967. This was 1980.

We noticed that few, if any, of the passengers appeared to be either Yugoslav or Romanian. Like ourselves, there were others heading for the conference in Bucharest, and there were black Africans. One of the latter who was fluent in English explained that he was a Nigerian medical student with funding to attend a Romanian university. He had had to spend his first year studying the Romanian language, and every summer he went to England to visit an aunt who lived there. While in England, he could examine medical textbooks, and he believed that the quality of his education in Bucharest was very good.

Around midnight, we approached the Yugoslav-Romanian border. Most European countries had exit controls, and cheerful Yugoslav officials checked our passports and wished us a good trip. Then we crossed the border, where we waited for what seemed an hour.

"They're putting ladders beside the train!" said Barbara. Evidently Ceauşescu feared that some undesirable might smuggle himself *into* Romania, and the guards were checking to see that that did not happen. Then I noticed a man in overalls crawling along the aisle and shining a flashlight under the seats, again to guarantee that nobody was hiding there. Did Ceauşescu fear terrorists, or was this his idea of a way to create employment? Given the number of uniformed police who patrolled the streets of Bucharest during our conference so that foreigners and Romanians could not fraternize, perhaps the answer to both questions was affirmative. What was certain was that such numbers in the security services meant fewer people to do productive work. Even in August, Romanians experienced a shortage of fruit.

Eventually the train moved out of the station, and a multilingual money-changer entered our section. ATMs had not yet become available, and in 1980 international tourists used travellers cheques, usually from American Express. Negotiable in most countries, they were a convenient way of dealing with possible theft. American Express had a well deserved reputation for replacing stolen ones quickly. In 1980, more than two decades before the Euro replaced most national currencies, it was customary to change some travellers cheques into the local currency when entering a country, enough to manage for a few days, and then to make further conversions as the need arose. The Konareks had their travellers cheques in Canadian dollars, Gwynneth in U.S. dollars, we in West German Deutschmarks.

For some reason, the moneychanger decided to deal with all five of us at once. We signed in the appropriate places and handed him the cheques; he in turn gave us piles of lei, the Romanian currency. Barbara, who had a hand-held calculator, quickly determined that he had been much too generous and invited him to sit down and redo his calculations. Regarding her as a nuisance, the man was anxious to deal with the remaining passengers.

Barbara was a professional school teacher, and at that point, she demonstrated her authority. She told him so firmly to sit down with us that he did. Then *she* did the arithmetic and showed him his mistake. When the man saw the size of the error, he made the sign of the cross!

Ten days later, we flew from Bucharest back to Yugoslavia. Train travel in one direction was an adventure. In both directions it would have been an ordeal. Airport security took place at the entrance to Bucharest airport, and only people with the appropriate documentation could enter the building. Family members could not accompany loved ones who might be leaving. When we boarded our Air France flight, where French law prevailed even as we sat on the ground, there was an assortment of international magazines and newspapers. Within Romania, only Romanian literature had been available, even at our conference.

The book stalls displayed little except books supposedly written by Ceauşescu or about Ceauşescu. He even managed to star in a history of the Romanian Orthodox Church. More than ever, the five of us could appreciate how privileged we were to be in a position to cross the Romanian border on an outbound flight.

Note

1. In August 1989, I visited Budapest, where Hungarian political parties had booths promoting their causes in the forthcoming parliamentary elections, the first multi-party elections in decades. One exhibit had a map which emphasized Hungary's "lost" territories, which included much of the former Habsburg Empire.

Chapter 6

Latin American Borders

There have been some memorable moments at Latin American borders. The one on the highway between the Guatemalan city of Chiquimula and the Honduran archaeological site of Copán was labour-intensive to say the least. When friends and I made a same-day return trip in May 1977, there were three teams of men, each stationed about one kilometre apart, on both sides of the line. One person asked the questions—the same questions at each stop—and wrote the answers onto a piece of paper on a clipboard. The rest stood silently beside the questioner. When we returned that afternoon, the heavens had opened and the rain was, literally, tropical. Everyone simply waved us through!

The actual border on the highway between Bariloche, Argentina, and Osorno, Chile, sits high in the Andes on a frozen wasteland marked only by a statue of the Virgin Mary at the actual spot. Both customs offices occupy sites at lower, more comfortable elevations. As we entered Chile in March, 1997, officials pulled every piece of luggage from the bus and X-rayed it. Chilean authorities wanted to protect their country's fruit industry and did not want harmful viruses from elsewhere. After the lengthy procedure, there was a request to all passengers to tip the customs officers. Taking to heart advice from the Chicago economist Milton Friedman, the government of Augusto Pinochet (1973-1990) had stopped paying the customs officers, and the requester said that the officers' incomes depended upon voluntary contributions from those of us being searched. How susceptible to bribery must those officers be?

The most memorable Latin American border crossing, however, has to be that along the border between Argentina and Brazil in 1988. Rupert Cook was a

Professor of Economics at Laurentian University, and his wife Elisabeth taught in the English Department. Rupert came from England, Elisabeth from Wales, but they had moved to Canada in 1967 and raised their children as Canadians. Rupert and Elisabeth loved Mardi Gras and waterfalls, and went to as many as they could. Canadian universities (other than those located in Quebec) suspend classes for a week each February. The official name for the occasion is "Reading Week," probably because "February break" is too polysyllabic. Many use that week for tropical vacations. In 1988, Reading Week coincided with Mardi Gras, and we went to Río de Janeiro with the Cooks and with Helen Devereux from Laurentian's Anthropology Department.

We arrived in Río on an overnight Saturday-Sunday flight. By definition, Mari Gras climaxes on Tuesday and disappears completely with the arrival of Ash Wednesday. For entertainment the rest of the week, we arranged a side trip to Iguazú Falls,[1] located where Argentina, Brazil, and Paraguay converge. Our Varig aircraft landed at Foz do Iguaçu, the community on the Brazilian side of the river, and Erno, the driver of the minibus which took us to our hotel, was eager to take us sight-seeing. We asked him to let us explore the Brazilian side of the falls on foot but accepted his offer of a trip the next day to the Itaipú Dam on the river which separates Brazil from Paraguay and to Puerto Presidente Stroessner (since Stroessner's fall in 1989, known as Puerto del Este) in Paraguay. Crossing the river into Argentina was another matter. I explained that Brazil was charging Canadians $75 for visas, but that people travelling on British passports could visit Brazil without any such payment. Under the circumstances, Rupert and Elisabeth were using British passports, and British passports might be problematic in Argentina. The Falklands War of 1982 was fewer than six years behind us, and Margaret Thatcher—the great British protagonist at the time—was still the British Prime Minister.

Erno responded, "Leave it to me. Everything will be all right."

Promptly at the agreed time, Erno arrived the next morning. We piled into his minibus and drove to the Itaipú Dam. As Canadians, we were interested in language usage in a border area. Our hotel and other tourist places on the Brazilian side of the river had signs in Portuguese and English, but never in Spanish. Indeed, according to Erno, the schools in Paraná—which includes Foz do Iguaçu—did not teach Spanish. Yet, Erno confirmed my guess that Brazilians were much more likely to learn Spanish than Argentines and Paraguayans were to learn Portuguese. Later in the day, we saw no Portuguese-language signs in the border regions of either Paraguay or Argentina.

The Itaipú Dam across the Paraná River was truly a marvel. Eight kilometres in length, it was, said the guide, the world's largest—larger than the Grand Coulee Dam in the United States or Krasnoyarsk in what was then the Soviet Union. In 1973, the Brazilian and Paraguayan governments had concluded the Treaty of Itaipú, which established the rules. It started to produce electricity in 1984, with each partner entitled to half. As Paraguay did not need its entire entitlement, it sold the surplus to Brazil, and the dam provided electricity for much of southern Brazil. The name "Itaipú," the guide said, means "Sound of the rocks in the river" in the Guarani language. The planners thought of more than electrical production. An anthropological museum displayed artifacts taken from the area about to be flooded, and a game sanctuary had become home to animals rescued from the rising waters.

From the Brazilian side of the Itaipú Dam, Erno then drove us to Puerto Presidente Stroessner, a very modern-looking city. Brazilian shoppers with empty suitcases jammed the lanes of the bridge *to* Paraguay, while returning Brazilians with loaded suitcases walked and drove the other way. Buses from the Foz do Iguaçu went to Puerto Presidente Stroessner, and cars on the bridge had both Brazilian and Paraguayan licence plates. The traffic was so heavy that pedestrians had the advantage of speed. Paraguayan Customs waved us through, but we witnessed what we thought was the driver ahead of us passing a bribe through the window of his car.

Prices throughout Puerto Presidente Stroessner were in Brazilian currency, and imports of every description from Europe and Asia were available. As Paraguay lacked industry of its own, it imposed no duties on those goods, which were then available at lower price than in Brazilian and Argentine stores. Some of the merchandise was junk. Joan bought what was supposed to be French perfume, but it turned out to be coloured alcohol. There was also a busy postal desk where tourists, including ourselves, could write postcards and mail them with Paraguayan stamps.

When we returned to Brazil, we did not have to show our passports. The Brazilian officer saw us, said "Foreigners?" to Erno, and on receiving an affirmative reply waved us on. Neither Brazil nor Paraguay had departure formalities.

Then came the moment of truth—the trip to Argentina. Never before had I been involved, even indirectly, in smuggling illegal aliens across an international border, and never had the Cooks been in such a position. In 1978, they had been refused permission to cross the border from Belize (previously known as British Honduras), which Guatemala claimed, into Guatemala, but they had remained on the Belizean side of the border. Everyone except Erno was somewhat nervous, and Elisabeth told a story.

"When Rupert was younger and living in England," she said, "he was a very good soccer player. One day the league schedule required the team to play a game in Wales. One of the players was a South African with a great capacity for soccer but limited knowledge of political science. His team mates decided to play a practical joke on him and gave advance notice to the bus driver so that he would co-operate.

"This was the era of *apartheid*. As the bus approached the Welsh border," Elisabeth continued, "the team mates advised the South African that Wales had closed its borders to South Africans. Therefore, he had to hide. The bus stopped short of the border, and the South African climbed into the bin behind the luggage.

"At the border, the bus stopped for what the players pretended was a customs inspection. From his hiding place in the bin, the South African could hear voices as the phoney customs officers asked questions. An 'officer' opened the bin and prodded the luggage. He then closed the bin, and the bus drove into Wales. Some distance inside Wales, the bus stopped, and the South African was allowed out of the bin and back into his seat.

"The poor man did not realize that this was a joke," said Elisabeth, "for as the bus approached the Welsh-English border on the homeward trip, the South African suggested that it was time for him to return to his hiding place." All of us wondered what Erno might have in mind for the Cooks.

The border crossing was simplicity itself. We crossed the Iguazú River on the Tancredo Neves Bridge, named for the President-elect who had won Brazil's 1985 election but died before his inauguration. The Argentine officials knew Erno, who said in Spanish, "Cinco Canadienses!" (Five Canadians!). The Argentines waved us forward. Minutes later, Erno stopped his vehicle so that we could photograph a billboard, "Las Malvinas son Argentinas!" (The Falkland Islands belong to Argentina!). We shopped in the border town of Puerto Iguazú, where the merchandise consisted of such Argentine specialties as fur and leather goods. We also visited Iguazú National Park on the Argentine side of the river.

There we encountered the challenge. Fortunately, the park attendant came to *me*, although if he had gone to Rupert, Rupert probably would have directed him in my direction as I could speak Spanish and Rupert could not. The officer had a register of guests who had visited the park, and there were spaces for our names, nationalities, and passport numbers. I flaunted my Canadian passport, then wrote my name and number. In a loud voice I asked Joan and Helen for theirs, and wrote their names and numbers. Then I whispered to Rupert, "Keep your passport hidden, but give me a number." He obliged, and a few minutes later we left Argentina without incident but with the Cooks.

After Margaret Thatcher's retirement, the situation eased. On sabbatical in 1996-1997, I spent the first few months of 1997 in Chile, researching a book about that country's performance during World War II. The Cooks came for a visit, and together we went to Argentina, this time openly and honestly. The United Kingdom still possessed the Falkland Islands, and the government of Argentina still claimed them. Argentine weather forecasts included "Las Malvinas" along with other parts of the country, and maps showed "Las Malvinas" as an integral part of Argentina. However, tensions had eased, and British tourists were welcome. By 1997, whatever problems there were, were with their government, not with individual British subjects.

Note

1. *Foz do Iguaçu* in Portuguese, *Cataratas de Iguazú* in Spanish.

Chapter 7

Inter-German Borders in the Year of Revolutions (1989)

In 1848, European countries from the Pyrenees to the Vistula had political up-heavals. Even tiny Monaco lost five-sixths of its territory. There were no major international wars, but there were major changes in the forms of government in such important capitals as Copenhagen, Paris, and Vienna. German revolutionaries of 1848 had failed to make their homeland more democratic, with consequences for the entire world. Places as remote as the United States, Australia, and temperate South America underwent major changes as German refugees landed on their shores and became citizens.

The only comparable year since then has been 1989, when fortuitously, I was beginning my third sabbatical from Laurentian University. Planning for a successful sabbatical takes years, and when Joan and I began to plan an around-the-world expedition with most of it in Europe, we had no idea that such major developments would happen while we were there. Before we left Canada in mid-summer, the Hungarian government had already removed the physical Iron Curtain which separated Hungary from Austria. The barbed wire and guard dogs were no longer there. That summer, Poland elected its first post-Communist government, and Soviet leader Mikhail Gorbachev indicated that it would be free to assume office. Thousands of East German "tourists" flooded into West German Embassies in Budapest, Prague, and Warsaw to seek political asylum and residence in West Germany, and more went on camping vacations around Hungary's Lake Balaton near the Austrian border and refused to return home. In September, the Hungarian government let them cross *en masse* into Austria, from which they drove to new homes in West Germany. When the East German government then forbade its people from going to Hungary, they flooded into Czechoslovakia and headed straight for the West German Embassy in Prague. Afraid that Czechoslovakians might get ideas, the Czechoslovakian government opened its northwestern border to East Germans so that they could go to West Germany. The East German politburo realized that the so-called German Democratic Republic (East Germany's official name) faced a mass exodus if its citizens believed that they could make a once-for-all dash for freedom via another European country. On 9 November, it opened the inter-German border, and in 1990 permitted multi-party elections. A party pledged to union with West Germany won, and in fewer than nine months after the opening of the Berlin Wall, the German Democratic Republic was history.

Before leaving Canada, we bought a Saab from a dealership in Ottawa which had experience selling to diplomats and military personnel who would be staying in Europe for at least a year. The supplier in Sweden's second largest city, Goteborg, would be waiting for us 10 August. The gateways to Sweden from Western Europe were Denmark and Berlin, and we decided to go there via Berlin, when we had no car, and to return via Denmark with the car. We would stay in West Berlin (occupied by soldiers from the United States, the United Kingdom, and France) because it was more familiar and required far less red tape than an overnight stay in East Berlin, capital of East Germany.

The morning of Friday, 4 August, Joan, our younger son Andrew (age 11), and I boarded the train for Berlin at the Hook of Holland, where the North Sea ferry arrives from Harwich, England. It had coaches from three countries—the Netherlands, West Germany, and East Germany. One official told us to sit in one of the East German coaches, because they were the only ones which would be going all the way to Berlin. If possible, the plumbing was even worse than that on the Romanian train, and the stench made it something between undesirable and impossible to sit anywhere near the washrooms. When we had to relieve ourselves, we went into a Dutch or West German coach. We made a mental note to visit the W.C. before Helmstedt, the last place in West Germany before the inter-German border, where we assumed that the Dutch and West German coaches would be detached. In 1989, the train required three hours to cross the Netherlands, four hours for West Germany, and another three for the ninety miles (150 kilometres) from Helmstedt to West Berlin, considerably longer than on the post-unification express trains of the late 20th century. Alas! To our horror, after Hanover—well to the west of Helmstedt—the only coaches remaining were the East German ones, and we had a rather uncomfortable ride for the last few hours.

East Germans managed the dining car, and one sign underlined the failure of that country, months as it was from collapse. "Citizens of the German Democratic Republic," it said, "can pay for their meals in the currency of the German Democratic Republic. All others must use convertible [Western] currency." East Germany must have been one of the few countries in the history of the world to refuse payments in its own currency.

As we approached Helmstedt, West German passport officers asked to see our passports. They left the train there, and the train pulled ahead into Marienborn, East Germany. Between Helmstedt and Marienborn, we saw a fence through a field, with a ploughed strip running its length and watchtowers at intervals. Once inside East Germany, we found the tracks enclosed by fences and watchtowers until Marienborn. However, nobody came crawling through the train to look for illegals under the seats, and nobody raised ladders to observe the train's roof. (Presumably one could do this from the watchtowers). East German passport control officers and ticket-takers processed us while the train was moving. The officer who provided transit visas insisted that passengers must remove sunglasses so that he could scrutinize their faces and guarantee that they matched the passport photos, but contrary to what we had heard, he was efficient and pleasant. After all, it was 1989!

At the time, I considered the East German border inspection little more than a "make-work" project. Except for pauses in Marienborn so that the East German officials could board and in Griebnitzsee southwest of Berlin to let them off the train, the train was going non-stop from West Germany to West Berlin. There was no opportunity for an East German dissident to board, nor for an undesirable to leave. However, when I flew from Vancouver to Sydney (Australia) in July 2002, I discovered that the U.S. Government no longer had in-transit facilities for those at the Hawaiian refueling stopover who were making a trans-Pacific flight. *All passengers* had to undergo an inspection by U.S. Immigration as though they were intending to stay in the United States for six months. Admittedly, an airliner can be a more lethal weapon than a train, but the government of George W. Bush shared in common with the East Germany government of Erich Honecker a desire to check first-hand the identity of everyone on its territory.

There was no charge for the transit visa, and no official returned for a second inspection before we left East Germany for West Berlin. Shortly after Griebnitzsee we had our first glimpse of the Berlin Wall and passed into the West Berlin suburb of Wannsee, where sailboats were out on the lake and their owners were taking advantage of a fine summer's day. Suddenly, the buildings became more attractive than their East German counterparts, and there were more people. We stopped at Wannsee so that some passengers could leave, then headed for Bahnhof Zoo, the station in downtown West Berlin.

The following day (Saturday), we walked along the West Berlin side of the Wall from Checkpoint Charlie, the crossing for vehicular traffic, to Potsdamer Platz and the Brandenburg Gate. The atmosphere was relaxed, as it had appeared to be along the platform at the Helmstedt station the previous afternoon. By 1989, nobody anticipated a Communist invasion. We discovered that the East Germans had actually built two walls, one near the line separating the Soviet sector from the American, British, and French sectors, the other more deeply inside East Berlin, East Germany's capital. The area between the two walls was a nomansland. Apart from watchtowers with guards, there were no buildings and no people.

There was no tension. At Checkpoint Charlie, there was a hot dog stand, and we could go right to the boundary to take pictures. We could and, like everyone else did, walk along a narrow stretch of *de facto* nomansland—the one untidy part of Berlin—between the Wall and the line which separated the Soviet and Western sectors. The Soviets and East Germans had abandoned a strip a few metres in width between the Wall and their sectoral boundary.

North of the Brandenburg Gate (a few metres inside East Berlin) and the restored Reichstag or Parliament Buildings (a few metres inside West Berlin) was the River Spree, which at that point formed the sectoral boundary. Signs on the West Berlin side of the canal warned that the water's edge marked the border. In other words, nobody should dive into or swim in that part of the river. The East Germans had a police boat which did not move. Its occupants must have had a succession of boring days, hoping that nothing would happen on their watch so that there would be no "need" to shoot but nevertheless waiting for something untoward to happen.

Later in the day we took a train ride on Line 2 of the S-Bahn (Strassebahn or street railway), Berlin's elevated urban railway. Line 2 began and ended in

West Berlin but cut across a corner of East Berlin, parallelled the Wall, and for a stretch even ran between the inner and outer Walls. The East Berlin section included five stations, but the train stopped at only one, Friedrichstrasse, where East Germany had border controls. Those who left or entered the train there had to deal with East German officials, while those of us who remained on the train were not checked. Somebody must have decided that it was simpler to close the other four stations than to have five centres for border control within a few blocks of each other.

City maps showed that the two Berlins were the antitheses of each other. West Berlin had streets named for Konrad Adenauer, first Chancellor of West Germany; John Foster Dulles, U.S. Secretary of State for most of the 1950s; and 17 June 1953, the date of an East German revolt. East Berlin streets bore the names of German Communists: Karl Marx, the original Communist ideologue; Karl Liebnecht, the Communist revolutionary of the World War I era; and Otto Grotewohl and Wilhelm Pieck, early leaders of East Germany.

We spent Monday, 7 August, sightseeing in East Berlin. As Canadians, we could do so with little difficulty. First we took S-Bahn line 3 from the Bahnhof Zoo in West Berlin to Friedrichstrasse in East Berlin. The short ride was one of the most memorable of our lives, over the wall with watchtowers and cleared areas beneath us. Signs at Friedrichstrasse directed us to passport control, where the officials politely sold us day visas and 25 East German Marks (none for Andrew, because of his age) which had to be spent before our departure from East Germany. Again, the officials carefully scrutinized our faces to guarantee that they matched the people in the passport pictures. We were supposed to divide ourselves into four categories: citizens of the German Democratic Republic (East Germany), citizens of the German Federal Republic (West Germany), residents of West Berlin (whom East German authorities refused to recognize as citizens of the German Federal Republic), and foreigners (such as ourselves). Most of the East Germans were senior citizens, pensioners, whose defection would have eased the burden on the East German treasury. Younger ones were less free to travel outside the Communist world, even to West Berlin, until they had repaid their debt to the society which had financed their education. Poles joined us in the line for foreigners, but unlike us they did not have to change their currency into East German Marks.

The only unpleasantness occurred when I sought to buy Wednesday's rail tickets to Sweden. The Information booth at Friedrichstrasse directed me to a certain room, where a woman told me to inquire elsewhere. After some time, I discovered that that woman actually *was* in charge of ticket sales outside the two Germanies, and when I returned to her she willingly sold the tickets. She did insist on charging full fare for Andrew, and when I asked about the train's time of departure, she was reluctant to say. Eventually she did, and she also said that it would leave from another East Berlin station, Lichtenberg, and provided a map of East Berlin's U-Bahn (underground railway) and S-Bahn network so that we could find our way there. Like the staff in the dining car of the train from the West to Berlin, she insisted that I must pay in *West* German Marks, not the local currency.

(From Zurich late in August, I wrote to complain about the fare charged for Andrew. Our refund reached us in June 1990, by which time East Germany no longer had a Communist government.)

From Friedrichstrasse station, we went onto the street of that name, a few blocks from Checkpoint Charlie. We inadvertently headed north into a colourless, even Spartan, section of East Berlin. Turning around, we retraced our steps to Unter den Linden, the centre of historic Berlin, then walked along that famous street and Karl Liebnechtstrasse past Marx-Engels Platz to the Alexanderplatz. This was showcase East Berlin.

Built like the Champs Elysées in Paris, Unter den Linden had the National Opera House—one of Europe's finest—on its south side, and the National Library, Humboldt University, and the monument to the victims of Fascism and militarism on the north side. Across the River Spree, Unter den Linden became Karl Liebnechtstrasse. Past Marx-Engels Platz on the south side was the Palace of the Republic, a glass structure which reflected the Lutheran Cathedral across the street. The Cathedral miraculously survived world War II when the rest of the neighbourhood was flattened, and in 1989 it was celebrating 450 years of Protestant Christianity in Germany. Along this stretch were cultural exhibits from Poland and Hungary, a huge bookstore, and the Pergamon Museum with its collection of Middle Eastern treasures.

Then we turned into the Alexanderplatz, East Berlin's principal shopping complex. Joan thought the merchandise adequate but inferior to that offered by K-Mart. The brand names were not familiar. She also considered the merchandise in stores along Unter den Linden somewhat better. The atmosphere at the Alexanderplatz was reminiscent of Expo '67 in Montreal, with the S-Bahn replacing the mini-rail, with many outdoor cafes, and large numbers of happy people.

We returned along Unter den Linden to the Friedrichstrasse station. We made frequent stops to try to spend the 50 East German Marks which we could not take back to West Berlin.

Our first restaurant, outside an elegant hotel at the corner of Unter den Linden and Friedrichstrasse (almost within sight of the Brandenburg Gate) served a lovely roast pork dinner. However, as in Romania in 1980, the waitress gave us a menu and let us order. Once we did, she said that there was only the one meal—pork. (Joan and I revisited that same restaurant in 2000, almost ten years after reunification. By then, it really did serve what its menu offered.)

We also stopped for delicious soft ice cream at a stand beside Unter den Linden. Only one flavour—chocolate—was available. Our impression was that what there was was fine, but variety was lacking. Ominously for the régime, East Germans could watch West German television and see what was available on the other side of the border. Cars in East Berlin included a few Western makes, but also Ladas (from the Soviet Union), Skodas (from Czechoslovakia), Trabants and Wartburgs. Trabants were so inferior to their Western counterparts that production ceased in May 1991, seven months after reunification. West Berlin advertised innumerable girlie shows, and *Playboy* was readily available, but we saw none of that in East Berlin. However, we did see one woman examining the garbage near Alexanderplatz and helping herself to some items, and we saw a lottery outlet.

At our final café, outside a hotel beside the Friedrichstrasse station, the waitress told us in English that East German children began to study Russian in Grade 5 and English in Grade 7, but that their English was better than their Russian because English was more similar than Russian to German and because there were more opportunities to practise. English-speaking tourists wandered around East Berlin, but Russian soldiers rarely did. Certainly we saw none.

As we re-entered the Friedrichstrasse station, people identified us as tourists, guessed that we wanted to go to West Berlin, and pointed in the appropriate direction. There seemed no resentment that we could go where they could not. Again, two officials who examined our passports, independently of each other, asked Joan to remove her sunglasses so that they could confirm her identity. Another noted that Andrew had not signed his passport, and he did so at once. We then gained admission to the S-Bahn platform, where there was a duty-free counter for passengers going to West Berlin. As the West Germans refused to recognize the sectoral boundary as an international frontier, there was no inspection on the West Berlin side. That enabled West Berliners to hop onto an S-Bahn to Friedrichstrasse, shop in the duty free facilities on the platform without going through the entry and exit formalities, then return to West Berlin with the purchases.

Wednesday we returned to East Berlin in order to catch the Sweden-bound train at the Lichtenberg station. Formalities this time at Friedrichstrasse were brief. We obtained our transit visas and did not have to change currency. I bought S-Bahn and U-Bahn tickets for the trip to Lichtenberg from a rude woman who rejected the 10 West German Marks which I offered her. (The price of rides in West Berlin had been 7.10 Marks.) On the assumption that she wanted East German currency, I went to another window to change 50 West German Marks. Heeding warnings from guide books, I turned town an offer of a black marketeer and changed at the official rate of 50 for 50. The teller gave two twenty notes, one five, and some coins. The ticket vendor then took only 1.50 Marks for our fare. Evidently, she had rejected the original offer because she did not want to make change for ten Marks. In turn, I wondered whether we could possibly spend 48.50 East German Marks between East Berlin and East Germany's Baltic port, Sassnitz.

Trains to Hungary, Czechoslovakia, Romania, Poland, and other points in East Germany arrived and departed as we awaited our Swedish connection at Lichtenberg station. On another platform, a group of chanting youths, presumably Young Pioneers—more common in East Germany than Boy Scouts and Girl Guides—marched and sang on another platform before boarding a train to Warsaw. Despite the "No Smoking" signs, people smoked. The newstand sold *Rude Pravo* from Czechoslovakia, *L'Humanité* from Paris, and other Communist newspapers from Soviet bloc countries, but nothing else.

Aboard the train, the conductor suggested that we move to the last coach, the only one of the twelve on the train which would actually cross the Baltic and go to Sweden. The coach served bottle drinks and a kind of cheeseburger on rye bread. It accepted East German money, but spend as a might, I still had a surplus of 30 marks (Canadian $22) when we reached Sassnitz. I asked a border control official who entered our coach what to do with the surplus money, and she exchanged our East German money into West German. Andrew said something about "East German money," and an official snarled, "German Democratic Republic money!" Andrew waited until the official was out of earshot, then said, "Any country that builds a wall to keep its people from travelling is not democratic." I was proud of him.

As in East Berlin, the border police at Sassnitz checked carefully to make certain that we (and everyone else) matched the pictures in our passports. By this time, Joan automatically removed her sunglasses before being asked. Yet, at no point did anyone search our luggage.

My parting thought was that while the so-called German Democratic Republic was certainly not democratic in our sense of the word, it certainly was German. We were unaware of seeing a single Soviet citizen, solder or civilian. Whatever the East Germans were doing, they were doing to themselves.

Chapter 8
The Austro-Hungarian Border in 1989

Until the Treaty of Trianon formally ended World War I in 1919, Austria and Hungary were the heart of the Habsburg Empire. The Treaty of Trianon dictated the new border, sixty to eighty kilometres east of Vienna, and that boundary assumed unprecedented importance with the withdrawal of Soviet forces from Austria in 1955 and the Soviet invasion of Hungary the following year. Thirty-three years later, both Soviet and Hungarian leaders had become less ideological and more tolerant, and early in 1989, Hungarian removed the physical barriers between Austria and Hungary. The first President George Bush "rewarded" the Hungarian government with a visit to Budapest later that spring. Nonetheless, in 1989 citizens of NATO countries still required visas in order to visit Hungary, and although we saw cars from Poland and Hungary on Austrian highways, even one from Bulgaria, we saw none from East Germany.

Taking the advice of the landlady at our bed-and-breakfast outlet in Vienna, I spent hours at the Hungarian Embassy in Vienna in order to purchase our Hungarian visas. "Tomorrow is Saturday," she warned, and huge crowds of weekend campers on their way to Lake Balaton will be pushing and shoving to buy visas at the border." I had to pay extra for same-day service, but it was well worth the price. Despite this precautionary move, which undoubtedly saved six to eight hours, we needed six hours for the 330 kilometre drive from Vienna to Budapest, eighty kilometreswithin Austria and the rest in Hungary.

Apart from the last thirty kilometres into Budapest, there was only a two-lane highway, and it was filled to capacity. Thousands of cars converged on the border, where we had to wait between two and three hours for what turned into casual processing. (There were no exit formalities for leaving Austria; the delay was entirely on the Hungarian side, although the line stretched back into Austria.) Warned about the quality of gasoline in Communist countries, I had filled the Saab before leaving Vienna, confident that 60 litres would take us from Vienna to Budapest and back into Austria with some surplus for sight-seeing in Hungary. I had not anticipated hours of idling at the border which left us so bereft of fuel that I feared we might have to park the car upon arrival in Budapest and save what was left for the return trip. Other motorists had a worse problem. Some idled so long that they used all their gasoline, and passengers literally had to push their cars across the border.

Inside Hungary, it was a relief to find that Shell had a network of service stations. Gasoline sold by Shell would be worthy of the brand name, I thought. Unfortunately, there was another problem. In 1989, Canada and the United States were making the transition from leaded to non-leaded fuels. The Canadian and US governments warned suppliers such as Saab that cars destined for the North American market should take only unleaded fuel. When we purchased the car from the factory at Goteborg, the Saab dealer warned us that under no circumstances should we use leaded fuel. There would be permanent evidence, he warned, and when the car reached Halifax, Canadian Customs would certainly check to see whether we had cheated. If we had, Canadian Customs would not release the car until the vehicle underwent a major reconstruction process—at our expense! Throughout Western Europe, most service stations offered a choice of leaded or unleaded fuel, and those which did not were not far from those which did. However, inside Hungary, Shell appeared to sell nothing but leaded fuel, which was useless for our purposes. Air pollution went hand-in-hand with Communist governments, and leaded fuel was a factor.

Our Hungarian host, Mr. Ruzkai, saved the day. Although he owned no car, Mr. Ruzkai remembered that there was a pump at the Swiss-owned Novotel in Budapest which sold unleaded fuel. He drove there with me, and that solved the problem. Mr. And Mrs. Ruzkai were helpful in many ways. They told us that the day of our arrival, Saturday, 19 August, was the day when runners in the Trans-Europe Marathon Race crossed the border from Hungary into Austria. An estimated 1000 East Germans camping near the border, presumably at Lake Balaton, dressed in t-shirts, shorts, and running shoes, and ran across the border with the Marathoners. Hungarian border officials pretended not to notice. Mr. Ruzkai guided us to the West German Embassy, where 200 East Germans had claimed political asylum and established residence. Mrs. Ruzkai said that the street and a nearby park had been full of East Germans who wanted to go to West Germany, but by the time of our arrival Sunday morning the situation was normal. Evidently they hade gone elsewhere, perhaps to Lake Balaton.

On Tuesday, 22 August, we drove from Budapest's heavily polluted air to Lake Balaton, where Czechoslovakian, French, German (both East and West), and other tourists camped, swam, and sunned themselves. The water was delightfully warm, and the beach and lake bottom were sandy. After a few hours of swimming and picnicking, we drove to Sopron, a classical Central European community from which the entire school of forestry—professors and students—had fled in 1956. From their refugee camp on the Austrian side of the line, they had relocated en masse in Vancouver at the University of British Columbia. From Sopron we crossed the border into Klingenbach, Austria, and drove the remaining less than sixty kilometres to Vienna.

This border crossing, in contrast to Saturday's, lasted but a matter of minutes, in part because Tuesday traffic was lighter than Saturday's but also because we were not using the main Vienna-Budapest highway. It was a hot day, and we had retracted part of the Saab's roof. At the Hungarian border post, Andrew stood, and when he popped through the roof, the friendly Hungarian officer laughed and shook his hand. Yet, that same officer insisted that we must open the trunk. We did, and he took a stick and poked vigorously. If we had been hiding anyone, East German or otherwise, the hidden passenger would certainly have reacted. By contrast, once we crossed the border, the Austrian Immigration Officers did not bother to examine our passports.

We formed several impressions. The Austrian properties appeared more prosperous, better painted, and better groomed than those inside Hungary. Within an hour of the border, we had seen Hungarians raking hay by hand, but Austrian agriculture was completely mechanized. More important, because Austrian cars were well maintained and, in many cases, designed for lead-free fuel, Vienna's air was immeasurably cleaner than that in Budapest. It was not as miserable an experience to drive behind a truck in Austria as to do so in Hungary. Budapest had a beautiful setting and beautiful architecture, much of it dating from the years when Austria and Hungary were part of the same empire and shared the same emperor, and many Hungarians owned their own cars, even if Ladas (from the Soviet Union), Skodas (from Czechoslovakia), Trabants (from East Germany), and Dacias (from Romania). Unfortunately, their technology was from the 1950s, and Budapest's environment was less than a match for that of Vienna, the other Habsburg capital on the Danube. The border, and the political systems on different sides of the border, made a significant impact.

Chapter 9

The Inter-Irish Border and the Irish Republican Army

Unfortunately, 1989 did not bring improvements along the Inter-Irish border. The Irish Republican Army (IRA) continued to explode bombs within Northern Ireland and along the inter-Irish border in the hope that they might blast the British off the island. The logic was that British soldiers and the British public would become weary of the ongoing violence and leave Northern Ireland to be absorbed into the Republic of Ireland. The government of Ireland did not approve of such measures, but the IRA had its own agenda.

By 1989, the current round of IRA violence had been taking place for twenty years. Unless there was massive destruction or multiple deaths, the outside world did not consider IRA violence newsworthy, and the international media (including the Canadian media) said little about it. There was no such silence within the Republic of Ireland and Northern Ireland, for the violence affected the daily lives of ordinary people. On 26 July, three days after our arrival in the Republic of Ireland, RTE (Radio-Television Eire, the counterpart of the CBC in the Republic of Ireland) reported the suspension of rail service between Dublin and Belfast because of a bomb threat. Every day RTE reported violence or the threat of violence either inside Northern Ireland or along the inter-Irish border. On 29 July, RTE reported another closing of the Belfast-Dublin rail line because of a bomb threat. RTE also reported a bomb at Newry, on the Northern Ireland side of the inter-Irish border on the line between Belfast and Dublin. On 31 July, RTE reported that rail service between Dublin and Belfast had resumed but that a road had closed because of terrorism. On 1 August, RTE reported an explosion on a rail line. Fortunately, the train was running late or the damage could have been extensive. *The Irish Independent*, a Dublin newspaper, reported that same day that there had been twenty-seven terrorist attacks and thirty-two bomb hoaxes on the Dublin-Belfast thus far in 1989. A friend in Belfast assured me that such disruptions were not at all unusual, and on 2 August *The Irish Independent* carried an editorial entitled "The Oppressor," which condemned the probable orchestrators of the violence, the Provisional Wing of the IRA (known colloquially as "the Provos"):

> The campaign to close down the Dublin to Belfast rail link is an example of the Provos' indifference to the views of the people they claim to represent. The British government will not suffer if that rail line is closed. But ordinary men and women will. Jobs will be jeopardised if users of the line move to other forms of transportation. Do the Provos care? Not one bit.
>
> It does not seem to have worried them that a train with 31 people aboard was nearly caught in one of those bomb attacks. It concerns them not one whit that a bomb outside Belfast's High Court could have caused untold horrors among civilians...Thousands of people in the North live lives which are conditioned by the threat of a bombing or shooting at any moment. This is oppression.

Regardless of the rights and wrongs of Irish history, regardless of whether there should have been a partition of Ireland in 1920 and if so whether British authorities had placed the inter-Irish border in the appropriate place, innocent people were suffering inconvenience, even death. I became convinced that the IRA had greater support among descendants of Irish famine refugees of the 1840s who were living in the United States and financing weapons purchases than among Irish people, regardless of religious persuasion, who had to live with the consequences of the violence.

After a few days in the Republic of Ireland, where I was collecting information for an article, I left that island and did not return until October, this time to Northern Ireland as well as the Republic of Ireland. In Belfast we stayed with friends, Dorothy Reid and Helen Gaston. One day Dorothy and Helen drove us to Northern Ireland's second city, not far from the inter-Irish border, known to the Protestants as "Londonderry" and to Roman Catholics as "Derry." It is a walled city, and with its eighteenth century buildings could have been a tourist attraction like Quebec City. Unfortunately, the effects of the violence were all too obvious. Barbed wire and barricades kept people from walking along the wall above the gates, presumably in case they might toss something onto passing traffic. Every building had metal security blinds, and stained glass was missing from St. Columb's Cathedral and St. Augustine's Church, both Church of Ireland (Anglican). A man from the cathedral told me matter-of-factly, "The last bomb [at the cathedral] had gone off in January or February." Evidently such happenings were so routine that he could not remember the date more precisely than that. Rebuilding was already under way.

Wherever we went, there were cement walls and road blocks around police stations. Twice we crossed the inter-Irish border, once north of Londonderry at Muff, once across the Foyle River which separates Strabane in Northern Ireland from Lifford in the Republic of Ireland. The British had nobody *at* the actual border; an officer would have been vulnerable to a raid from the other side. However, *inside* Northern Ireland side near Muff, perhaps a mile from the border, the British Army could check traffic from within a brick enclosure. At Strabane there were men of the Royal Ulster Constabulary (RUC), guns drawn, making spot checks. Military people who passed us, army or RUC, always wore camouflage and had tommyguns ready for action.

Strabane was a pretty town with an economy based on textiles and agriculture. Although we saw Church of Ireland and Presbyterian Churches there, the Roman Catholic section of this border community was highly memorable. Tricolour flags (of the Republic of Ireland) flew everywhere on the *Northern Ireland* side of the river, and artists had painted elaborate political messages onto the walls of attractive homes: "British Out of Ireland" and "You can kill the revolutionary but not the revolution." There was a quotation from the 1981 IRA hunger striker Bobby Sands, now an IRA "martyr," across the street from a picture of Che Guevara. A sign on the wall noted "Yassir Arafat, PLO, Libya." Libya's notorious leader, Colonel Muammar Qaddafi, was an IRA sponsor, and IRA members saw parallels between the Palestine Liberation Organization and their own organization, both attempting to "liberate" territory. By contrast, nobody at Lifford bothered to fly *any* flags. Residents of the Republic of Ireland had already settled questions of identity and knew who they were.

A couple of days later, we drove from Belfast to Sligo, in the Republic of Ireland. As we passed through Cookstown in Northern Ireland, we encountered an army blockade on the main street. The soldiers wore their usual battle fatigues and had guns drawn. Next we came to Enniskillen, where a bomb had killed eleven people and wounded sixty-three during the Remembrance Day ceremony of 1987.[1] The bomb had exploded in a confined area, but the cenotaph itself survived. Signs warned that the centre of Enniskillen's shpping area was a security zone where nobody could leave a car unless someone remained inside it.

Barely ten miles (fourteen kilometres) further, we crossed the inter-Irish border, from Belcoo in Northern Ireland to Blacklion in the Republic of Ireland. Again, nobody questioned us or asked to see any identification. The police station in Belcoo, like its counterparts throughout Northern Ireland, was a fortress, surrounded by high concrete walls and cameras.

Across the border in counties Cavan, Leitrim, and Sligo, the standard of living appeared comparable with that inside Northern Ireland. The biggest differences were the lack of security, the bilingual signs (English and Irish), and the posting of distances in kilometres instead of miles. Our host and hostess at Sligo, Basil and Ethne Buchanan, had a modern and attractive ranch house in a prosperous ranching area. Basil, a Protestant from a Protestant family, was enthusiastic about life in the Republic of Ireland. He attributed the absence of border controls to the IRA. It could intimidate any officials who dared to ask questions, he explained. The IRA, in his opinion, was not as formidable around Belcoo/Blacklion as in Monaghan County south of Newry, on the corridor between Belfast and Dublin. That really was IRA country. Sligo was sufficiently far from the border than Basil had no problems. He estimated that he handled 4000 cattle each year.

Days later, I travelled by train from Belfast to Dublin. Across the street from the platforms at Belfast Central Station, someone had printed onto a wall:

BRIT	MURDERERS	WHO'S	WHO
UVF	D		
C	F		

"RUC" referred to the Royal Irish Constabulary, the police force of Northern Ireland. "UVF" and "UDF" referred to Protestant vigilante groups, the Ulster Volunteer Force and the Ulster Defence Force. Another sign, a short distance south of the station, described Sinn Fein, the political wing of the IRA, "Sinn Fein: Freedom, Justice, Peace."

South of Lisburn Station in County Down, Northern Ireland, we encountered Protestant graffiti: "Join the RUC." More graffiti on the same wall in that Protestant part of Northern Ireland said without comment, "UVF," South of Lurgan station, crosses in a cemetery indicated that we had entered another Roman Catholic part of Northern Ireland. The graffiti said, "Provos Rule" and "PIRA," references to the Provisional IRA, the most extreme IRA group. However, at Portadown station, some Protestant had painted onto a fence, "UDF" and "No Pope Here."

From the train, Newry was not a bad looking place. It resembled Truro, Nova Scotia, spread from a valley up converging hills. We had left Belfast at 5 p.m. and reached Newry, the last stop in Northern Ireland, one hour later. South of Newry, motor traffic on the highway which paralleled the tracks was backed up at what appeared to be a British Army checkpoint. A sign said, "No photographs to be taken in this area."

Between Newry and Dundalk, the first stop in the Republic of Ireland, there were no border formalities whatever. It was like crossing from Alberta to Saskatchewan. The train reached Dublin at 7:25 p.m., five minutes behind schedule.

The return trip to Belfast four days later, 27 October 1989, the Friday of Halloween weekend, was more eventful. As I entered Dublin's railway station, a man seated at a desk called upon me to sign a petition while RTE television cameras rolled. The petition called upon the governments of the Republic of Ireland and Northern Ireland to maintain rail service between Dublin and Belfast and to protect it from terrorist attacks. The railway employee at the desk explained that he feared that the frequent disruptions might prompt Northern Ireland Rail, which operated the trains, to save money by closing the rail line. All too often, passengers had to abandon their trains and cross the border by bus, and someone might consider it more economical to rely on buses all the time and for the entire distance. I was willing to sign, for even if I appeared on the evening news in full colour, I would be some distance away, beyond the reach of the IRA. The employee was much more vulnerable, and I asked him whether it might be dangerous to promote such a petition here.

"Yes," he replied, "but then it's dangerous to work here too."

The southbound train from Belfast, which I was about to board for its northbound return trip, pulled into the Dublin station two minutes of schedule, and most of the passengers signed the petition as they left. A security guard checked our luggage (but not our persons) with a metal detector before allowing us to board. A sign indicated that we could also be asked for identification, but as far as I could see, nobody had to produce any. The train left Dublin right on time, and at Dundalk, in the heart of IRA country along the inter-Irish border, those of us who looked out the window could see a vivid example of raw courage. As in Dublin, there was a sign inviting signatures on the petition for a crackdown on terrorism.

North of Dundalk and south of Newry, road blocks and metal fences beside the tracks indicated that we had returned to Northern Ireland. Otherwise, there was little indication. Again, no border official (Customs or Immigration officer) boarded the train. A uniformed security guard boarded the train at Newry and sat across the aisle from me until we reached Belfast's Central Station. He said that he rode trains between Belfast and Newry to look for unattended luggage or anything else of a suspicious nature. I pointed out that I had left some of my luggage on the shelf above his head, on *his* side of the aisle, because nobody has been sitting there between Dublin and Newry. Why had he not questioned me about it? He answered that he had assumed that the luggage was mine. He then complained that his employer, obviously a private security company, was not very reliable with its pay checks and that it owed him some back pay. Under the circumstances, I thought that Northern Ireland Rail was amazingly, even alarmingly, casual.

The security guard explained that the large number of bomb scares had led Northern Ireland Rail to purchase its own fleet of buses for transporting passengers, when necessary, across the border. It was more economical, he confirmed, for Northern Ireland Rail, which operated the trains between Belfast and Dublin, to own its own buses than to charter them on short notice. An hour north of Newry, the train reached Belfast's Central Station, and all of us passed through the Customs Post there. There was not a single official to lay eyes on us.

Note

1. Derek Lundy, *The Bloody Red Hand: A Journey through Truth, Myth and Terror in Northern Ireland* (Toronto: Alfred A. Knopf Canada, 2006), p. 12.

Chapter 10

The Border Between Zimbabwe and Mozambique

From Europe, Joan, Andrew, and I flew to Zimbabwe, the former Southern Rhodesia, where we spent the months of May and June, 1990. Black Africans had gained full control ten years earlier under the leadership of Robert Mugabe, who had not yet destroyed one of the continents's strongest economies. Not for another decade would he encourage goons to invade and seize commercial farms managed by people who knew how to farm. In 1990, the farms provided such an abundant food supply that Zimbabean agricultural exports earned foreign exchange. It would be another decade before Mugabe destroyed the farms and created a famine in what had been a bread basket.

Mozambique, which lay between Zimbabwe and the Indian Ocean, was not as fortunate. It was in the midst of a civil war between Renamo forces sponsored by the *apartheid* regime in neighbouring South Africa and the country's Frelimo government. ("Frelimo" is derived from the Portuguese words for "Liberation Front of Mozambique," "Renamo" from "National Resistance of Mozambique.")[1] Mugabe felt sympathetic toward, perhaps even a sense of obligation toward, Frelimo, which had granted political asylum to him between Mozambique's achievement of independence from Portugal in 1975 and Mugabe's victory five years later in Zimbabwe's one fair and free election. From anecdotal evidence, we knew that Zimbabwe's armed forces were assisting the Frelimo government to battle the Renamo forces, but Mugabe's tightly controlled media—the Zimbabwe Broadcasting Corporation and the daily newspaper, *The Herald*—said little about this. Both consistently referred to "the Renamo bandits," but apart from labelling Renamo as undesirable, there was no public indication that Zimbabwe was intervening in another country's civil war.

As a Professor of History who taught a course on the 20th century world, I wanted to see what I could first hand. For better or for worse, on 10 June 1990 I managed to persuade our dubious host, Derek Fulton, who years earlier had migrated from England to what was then Southern Rhodesia, to take Joan, Andrew, and me to the Zimbabwe-Mozambique border post near Mutare, the former Umtali. I had photographed the inter-German border and the Austro-Hungarian border (albeit from the Western side in both instances) and even taken pictures of Soviet soldiers in Budapest. I had photographed bombed and burned trucks and buses on Belfast's Falls Road after a weekend of IRA activity there. I had even signed a petition for a crackdown on the IRA and had done so under the glare of television cameras. I was clearly over-confident about my immunity from danger.

Derek drove into the parking lot, just short of the building which housed the Zimbabwean Customs Office. Zimbabwe had exit controls because no person was supposed to take its currency out of the country. I jumped out and began to photograph army vehicles, soldiers, and tents. A soldier approached and ordered me into the Customs Office building.

"Why were you taking pictures here?" he asked. "Don't you know that you are in a war zone?"

I decided that naïvete was the best defence. "No," I responded. "How could I know that? I thought that the war was in Mozambique, not Zimbabwe."

That stumped him for a minute. Then he continued, "What is your name?"

"Graeme Mount," I answered. "What is your name?"

"My name is none of your business," he said. Later I discovered that it was Moses Kadenga. "As for yours—Graeme Mount—I have never heard a name like that before. What were you doing yesterday?"

"I climbed Mount Inyangani." Mount Inyangani was Zimbabwe's highest peak, about 70 kilometres from the room where Kadenga was interrogating me. The climb was not difficult even for middle aged professors, and Derek, Joan, Andrew, and I—along with some Scandinavians—had climbed it the previous afternoon.

"That must be a figment of your imagination," said Kadenga. "I have never heard of Mount Inyangani."

He noticed my wallet and demanded that I hand it to him. As he began to remove the cash, I demanded a receipt. Together we counted the money. He wrote the value of the money on a sheet of paper, then took both the paper and the money into another room. I memorized the figure.

Having little else to do, he began to rifle through my wallet. "What's this?" he asked.

"That is my Sudbury hospital card," I said. "If I have to go to a hospital, I do not need to answer a bunch of questions. I simply hand the clerk the card."

"What's this?" he continued.

"That's my OHIP card," I explained. "OHIP is short for Ontario Health Insurance Plan. If I have to go to a doctor, I do not pay cash. Instead, I produce this card, and the government of Ontario—the Canadian province where I live—pays the bill."

"What's this?"

"That," I said, "is my Laurentian University insurance plan. I teach at Laurentian University. If I need drugs—oops, medicine—I pay only 35 cents. Manufacturers Life, the insurance company, pays the rest."

"There seems to be lots about health here," said Kadenga. "Are you sick most of the time?" I suspected that he was beginning to believe that I was a narcotics trafficker.

"No," I explained. In Canada it is customary for people to carry insurance to take care of everything when we get sick. Look," I continued. "Let's make a deal. Give me my money back, and I'll open the back of my camera and destroy the pictures which you don't want me to have. I'll go away and take no more pictures here."

By this time, he had decided, I must be a South African spy. "We're going to call the CIO."

The CIO was Zimbabwe's notorious Central Intelligence Organization. Back in the car, Derek heard rumours that it would be coming, and he was frantic. However, I did not know and gave an unexpected reply. "That's great," I said. "How soon can it be here?" I thought that the CIO would have some professional expertise and would cut the nonsense in no time.

Kadenga and another officer continued to search my wallet and found no evidence of any South African connection. They adjourned to another room, returned my wallet, and *all* my money. Kadenga shook my hand and said, "If we meet again, I hope we shall meet as friends." I could even keep the film with the forbidden pictures.

Although pleased that I could go, I felt sorry for people who lived in a country with an army staffed by such clueless officers. Zimbabwe was scenically beautiful with friendly people and a perfect climate, high enough to avoid extreme heat but close enough to the equator that it avoided frosts. Yet it had its downside.

Since then, peace has returned to Mozambique, and in 2007 its former president, Joaquim Chissano, won an award for leading Africa's most honest and competent government. Under Robert Mugabe, Zimbabwe has descended from Purgatory into Hell.

Note

1. For more information on the war between Frelimo and Renamo, see Bill Purves, *Living with Landmines: From International Treaty to Reality* (Montreal: Black Rose), pp. vii-xix, 123-160.

Chapter 11

The Borders of North Korea

In recent years, North Korea—officially the Democratic People's Republic of Korea (DPRK)—has gained a well deserved reputation as one of the world's rogue states. Like the people of Zimbabwe in recent years, North Koreans have experienced famine, and like Robert Mugabe, North Korea's two heads of state, Kim Il Sung (1947-1994) and his son Kim Jong Il (since 1994), have provided highly intrusive and less than competent government. Joan and I had opportunities to visit North Korea's southern border (with South Korea) in April 1999 and its northern one (with the People's Republic of China) in July 2006. A recent book confirms that while neither border is easily permeable, those North Koreans who dare to escape have a better chance at a safe arrival if they go north to China than if they go to South Korea.[1]

Our host in Seoul, South Korea's capital, was Donald Marleau. Donald had been a student in classes taught by both Joan and me at Laurentian University, and after graduation he had gone to South Korea to teach English. Later he remained there as a businessman. Donald knew that South Koreans had a very high regard for education and educators, and he managed to work miracles for us. Canadians who had lived in Korea or visited it frequently had found themselves unable to visit Panmunjom on the inter-Korean border because tours which they tried to book were invariably already full. Nevertheless, Donald managed to arrange such a tour for us. His standard response whenever he received a negative answer was to say, "My professors will be *so* disappointed."

The person at the other end of the telephone line would say, "Your professors? Oh! We'll find a space for *them*. Send them over."

On a warm, sunny Wednesday before 8:40 a.m., 28 April 1999, Joan and I appeared as instructed at Seoul's Lotte Hotel in the heart of the South Korean capital. We had been warned in advance not to wear shorts or jeans. Men with long or untidy hair and ear rings also were not welcome. North Korean soldiers with cameras might take our pictures, and under no circumstances should they be allowed to depict us as decadent Westerners. (When, seven years later, Joan and I actually saw North Korean civilians in the North Korean city of Sinuiju, many of them *were* wearing shorts.) Three buses were available to take us to Panmunjom, two exclusively for Japanese tourists and a third for yet more Japanese plus a group of us who understood English. Our "English" group included several Canadians, some Australians, a group from Colombia, and a Salvarorean. Our bus had two guides, a woman who spoke Japanese and a kindly father-like man who spoke English. Apart from drivers and guides, who received special clearance, no Koreans could take these tours for fear that one or more might spy for North Korea. We had to take our passports with us.

The bus left promptly at 9 a.m. and travelled through urban sprawl until 9:40. Ten minutes north of Koyang, it stopped for five minutes at the monument to 1500 soldiers from the Philippines who had fought in the Korean War. At 10:07, we passed an anti-tank wall, at which point it was forbidden to take pictures. North of the wall there were farms, low-rise houses, and the occasional apartment.

At 10:30 we had a 15-minute break at Munsan to see monuments to war correspondents who died during the Korean War and to Korean patriots who had died in border skirmishes in 1948 and 1949, before the actual Korean War of 1950-1953. Before every stop, the guide would say, "Alcoholic beverages are available at this stop, but *you* must not have any. We don't want anyone wandering by mistake into North Korea." Over the years, he said, there had been defectors from both sides: Soviet, Czech, Chinese, North Korean, South Korean.

Munsan, population 35,000, was and remains the northern terminus of South Korea's rail system. A sign marks the spot, although the right-of-way continues in anticipation of what the guide considered inevitable unification. (On 17 May 2007, symbolic trains moved in both directions across the inter-Korean border on tracks constructed on both sides to link the rail systems of North and South Korea. However, it appears that Kim Jong Il had allowed the border crossings in response to South Korean bribes.[2]) Munsan lay in the dead centre of the Korean peninsula, 220 kilometers south of North Korea's capital, Pyongyang, 450 from the Yalu River—North Korea's border with China.

Leaving Munsan's Unification Park, we drove to the Unification Bridge across the Imjingak River. From Unification Bridge to Camp Bonifas, a U.S. Army base named for an American soldier killed 18 August 1976 by North Koreans while cutting a tree near the Bridge of No Return across the inter-Korean border, we could take no pictures of the barbed wire and sandbags clearly visible outside the bus window.

At Camp Bonifas, where we could again take pictures, we ate with U.S. soldiers in their mess. Again, the guide warned us not to consume any alcohol. When we finished, we were free to go to the souvenir shop or to buy postcards or clothing to commemorate our visit a few minutes later to the Demilitarized Zone (DMZ). Outside the buildings were the flags of the United Nations, South Korea, and the sixteen other nations—including Canada—which had fought under the United Nations Command during the Korean War.

The souvenir shop housed a museum. One exhibit read:

On 23 November 1984 a Soviet citizen, Vasily Matuzok, escaped to the free world by crossing the military demarcation line at Panmunjom. A firefight broke out when North Korean guards pursued the defector across the line and fired at him and UN command guards. The ensuing battle lasted 30 minutes. One Joint Security Administration soldier [the combined U.S.-South Korean force which patrols the South Korean side of the border] was killed and one wounded; the North Korean side had three soldiers killed and five wounded. Matuzok was protected throughout and subsequently evacuated to Fort Kitty Hawk.

From the Museum, we went to the VIP room at Ballinger House, where Private First Class Nawara of the U.S. Army distributed a list of "do's and don'ts," which we had to date and sign. Some of the rules included the following:

- Prior to entering the Joint Security Area, each visitor…will receive a laminated guest badge which identifies him/her as an authorized guest of the United Nations Command. Guest badges must be warn on the upper left side of the outmost garment. Guest badges must be turned in prior to departure from Camp Bonifas.

- Fraternization, including speak or any association with personnel from the Korean People's Army/Chinese People's Volunteers...side is strictly prohibited.

- Visitors will not point, make gestures, or expressions which could be used by the North Korean side as propaganda material against the United Nations Command.

- The area and buildings (tan colored) under the military control of the Communist side will not be entered for any reason.

Private Hill of the United States Army then gave a history lesson and pointed out that Kaesong in North Korea was only 12 kilometres from the DMZ. Hill said that the south side of the boundary markers had words in English and Korean, while those on the north side were in Korean and Chinese. There were, said Hill, two villages in the DMZ. In South Korea there was Tae Song-dong, where people who lived there before 1953 could continue to live and farm. They paid no taxes and enjoyed excemption from military service. Tae Song-dong, which means "Freedom Village," had a church and a primary school. On the North Korean side was Kijong-dong ("Propaganda Village"), uninhabited and deserted except for maintenance crews which visit Kijong-dong but live elsewhere. Swiss and Swedish soldiers lived on the South Korean side of the DMZ. Until the end of the Cold War, soldiers from Poland and Czechoslovakia had lived on the North Korean side, but the North Koreans have since ordered their expulsion. Each side was trying to outdo the other by attaching enormous flags to increasingly high flagpoles.

Farmers in the DMZ, said Hill, could own 14-17 acres provided that they spend at least 240 nights per year in the area. Elsewhere, South Korean farmers averaged 2-4 acres.

The motto of Camp Bonifas is "In front of them all". Private Hill said that Vice President Al Gore, Speaker Newt Gingrich, Secretary of State Madeleine Albright, and Defense Secretary William Cohen had all paid visits. South Korean soldiers served in the area 26 months, U.S. ones for 12, and both must be bigger than the average soldier in their countries and must be without a police record. Because of their diet, Private Hill said, South Koreans were much bigger than the North Koreans opposite them.

Private Hill said that a 1998 defector from North Korea had said that all North Korean soldiers in the DMZ were officers. To date, the South Korean and

U.S. armies admitted to having discovered seven tunnels dug by North Koreans under the border.

As the tour bus headed toward the Demarcation Line, Private Hill pointed to the "famous one-hole golf course" at Camp Bonifas. *Sports Illustrated*, he said, labelled it "the most dangerous [golf course] in the world" as it was surrounded by minefields on three sides.

As we left Camp Bonifas at Checkpoint Bravo, the ban on pictures resumed and remained in effect until we had left the Joint Security Area and reached the DMZ. We saw three lines of defence between Camp Bonifas and the DMZ, all of which stretched right across Korea: (i) an anti-tank wall; (ii) a live minefield; (iii) a double chain-link fence, with guard posts every two to three metres.

A blue sign marked the southern border of the DMZ. We would not photograph its farmers nor Tae Song-dong Village. Private Hill pointed to various observation posts either side of the border. From two inside South Korea, it was possible to look seventeen to twenty-seven kilometres into North Korea on a clear day. We saw the site of the Quick Reactionary Force, which was supposed to be ready to come with incendiaries within 60-90 seconds of an alarm but which has responded in drills within 38.

United Nations (blue) and Communist (more grey than tan) buildings straddled the border, and we had signed a pledge not to enter the grey ones. A microphone wire separated North Korea and South Korea inside one UN building, and Private Hill said that the North Koreans could hear every words spoken in that building. North Korean soldiers outside their administrative headquarters and elsewhere looked very professional, and North Korean music reached us from Propaganda Village. Private Hill said that propaganda was often blared southward.

Private Hill said that in order to avoid incidents, each side gave the other advance notice of visits by tourists. While we were visiting the border area, South Korean Military Police stood facing the blue buildings—half exposed and half protected—looking north. Hill said that the South Korean Military Police wore sunglasses while standing at the border in order to intimidate the North Koreans.

The Bridge of No Return had that name because almost all trips in either direction were final. Prisoners of War passed south when the Korean War ended. Captain Lloyd Bucher and the crew of the *Pueblo*, a U.S. spy ship captured by North Koreans in 1968, also returned via that bridge.[3] When a South Korean philanthropist responded to famine in North Korea, 1001 cattle travelled north across the bridge. Perhaps the only exception was the entourage with former President Jimmy Carter, who drove from Seoul to Pyongyang via Panmunjom in 1994 and returned via the same route a few days later.[4]

Because there was supposed to be no shooting in the DMZ, the DMZ had become a haven for wildlife, especially cranes and deer. We saw several cranes.

The bus returned to Seoul via a different route, paralleling the Han Estuary, which forms the inter-Korean boundary northwest of the South Korean capital. The highway's eight lanes (four in each direction) paralleled barbed wire and a strip between the barbed wire and the Han River patrolled by sentries and dogs. On either side of the river we could see watchtowers. Farmers cultivated right to the border.

Each side had propaganda billboards facing the other. According to the guide, the North Korean signs read "Yankee, go home!" or "South Korea—land of chance!" South Korea boasted, "Automobiles in South Korea—already ten million!"

A little more than seven years later, from 4-7 July 2006, Joan and I saw North Korea's other border, the one with China. Accompanying us was Chen Hua, Chinese wife of Joan's brother Jim. By 2006, relations between North Korea and China were not good. A badly maintained North Korean freighter had gone where it should not have gone in Shanghai harbour and had to pay a fine of 30,000 yuan (US$3,747).[5] The U.S. Government had blacklisted the Banco Delta Asia in Macau, until 1999 a Portuguese enclave but since December of that year a Special Administrative Region (like Hong Kong) of the People's Republic of China, for laundering counterfeit U.S. dollars manufactured in North Korea. Chinese authorities blamed the North Koreans for hurting one of their banks.[6] Joan, Hua, and I went to Dandong (known as Antung during the Korean War) on the Chinese side of the Yalu River (Green Duck River).

The three of us arrived at the Dandong International Hotel, where Hua had made reservations on the intenet. The internet was out of bounds to people in North Korea on the other side of the Yalu River. Our rooms were on the 14th floor, but there was a fancy, yet inexpensive restaurant on the 23rd. We went there for lunch and had a sweeping view of the Yalu River and the Sinuiju region of North Korea. The difference between the two sides was startling. Dandong (in China, population 2.5 million) was bustling with high rises, construction, and vehicular traffic as far as we could see. On the North Korean side, one would have been hard pressed to find a building of more than three storeys, and the buildings appeared derelict. There were many smokestacks, almost none of them in use. Sinuiju was North Korea's *sixth* largest city, one-tenth the size of Dandong. A huge ferris well dominated the skyline at Sinuiju, as though to advertise what a fun place North Korea must be, but we never saw it move.

This, of course, was typical of what we had heard and read about North Korea. Propaganda Village looks impressive from Panmunjom, but nobody lives or works there. Boutros Boutros-Ghali, who served as United Nations Secretary General from 1992 until 1996, wrote in his memoirs that when he visited North Korea in December 1993, he drove for four hours from Panmunjom to Pyongyang along an excellent highway almost totally devoid of other traffic. From the highway Boutros-Ghali saw unoccupied factories, which he labelled "Potemkin."[7]

After lunch, we went to the bridge which the United States Air Force bombed 8 November 1950 and observed the parallel Sino-Korean Friendship Bridge which replaced it. The North Koreans had demolished their part of the bombed bridge, but the Chinese converted their section into a theme park. For a price, one could look at Sinuiju through telescopes, and on the Chinese shore, vendors sold such North Korean souvenirs as assortments of stamps and liquor.

We hired a motor boat which went close to the North Korean shore. Most North Koreans whom we observed appeared to be doing very little. Two men fished, but from shore. Indeed, during our three days in the area, we did not see a single North Korean boat depart from its moorings. There was some construction, but not nearly as much as in Dandong. We waved as we passed, and some North Koreans waved back. From visual observations alone, the people of Sinuiju *must* be aware that there is a more prosperous world outside North Korea's borders.

The Yalu River at Dandong/Sinuiju is about one kilometre in width. There are a few places where the water flows quickly, but on the whole it does not. If it freezes, as it did during the Korean War and the decades before global warming, desperate North Koreans can make their way to the Chinese side of the river. However, a waitress from the restaurant at the Dandong International Hotel told Hua that the Yalu River no longer freezes in winter.

Hua, Joan, and I watched traffic on the Sino-Korean Friendship Bridge. Much of the time there was none at all. From the remnant of the bombed bridge, we did manage to photograph a train entering North Korea. It had one automobile on a flatcar plus a dozen or so boxcars. *Every* truck returning to China from North Korea appeared empty. Enclosed trucks were riding high, as though they had no load, and flatcars with an open top definitely had no cargo.

We returned to the 23rd floor of the Dandong International Hotel, watched the sunset and observed as the lights came on. The Chinese side of the Yalu River was bright; the North Korean side was almost totally dark. Boutros Boutros-Ghali had commented on the darkness of buildings even in Pyongyang.[8]

Early the next morning (5 July 2007), China's English-language television channel, CCTV (Chinese Central Television) reported that North Korea launched three or four missiles, which dropped into the Sea of Japan. The launchings coincided with Independence Day celebrations in the United States.

After breakfast, the three of us found a taxi driven by Taxi Driver Qu (pronounced "Chew") who, by happy coincidence, had a father born in North Korea and a Chinese mother. Qu himself had driven cargoes of rice into North Korea and was quite willing to discuss the place. According to Qu, the police had a very high profile in North Korea. There were two currencies, one for "special people" and one for everyone else. This enabled the "special people" to shop in places off limits to most North Koreans. There were many secret police, said Qu, and with so many men in the army, women dominated North Korea's labour force. Qu told us that Chinese trucks would go to an unloading ramp in Sinuiju, where North Korean women unloaded them. The trucks then returned empty to China, as we had witnessed the previous day. At age 18, North Korean men join the army, and the army absorbed a disproportionate part of the food supply. He also said that the North Korean army kept reserves of rice in case of emergency; preservatives from China kept the rice from spoiling. Bribery was common. North Koreans, continued Qu, threatened that without bribes, they would make trouble. As it was, North Koreans regularly stole lights from Chinese trucks. Chinese truck drivers were limited as to where they could go in North Korea, and Chinese vendors knew better than to sell on credit. As soon as the goods arrived, he said, the North Koreans had to pay cash, usually in United States dollars. (This would explain why North Korea was counterfeiting U.S. currency.) According to

Qu, the North Koreans liked to purchase Chinese cars, trucks, and refrigerators. A Chinese émigré from Dandong currently living in Los Angeles told Joan in the restaurant of the Dandong International Hotel that North Koreans sold wood and fish to China.

For roughly an hour, Taxi Driver Qu drove us upstream to Hushan, on the Chinese side of the Yalu River. There we discovered that the border was not entirely unguarded. During more friendly days between North Korea and China, Chinese leader Mao Zedong had ceded some islands in the Yalu River to North Korea so that North Koreans could have some fertile, agricultural land. (Before the partition of Korea in 1945, most of the peninsula's agricultural lands lay in what would become South Korea.) Mao's successors rebuilt the Great Wall of China at Hushan in order to limit what North Koreans could occupy. From the Chinese shore of the Yalu, which by that point was only a few metres in width, we watched for half an hour as North Koreans with their flag approached. Unfortunately, before I could take the perfect picture, a Chinese officer ordered us to leave. Presumably officials from both sides were seeking to prevent North Koreans from illegally entering China. It was easy to imagine that in winter when the upper Yalu might freeze, it would not be impossible for North Koreans to bribe a North Korean border guard and cross when the Chinese were not looking. (Except for problems related to border guards, swimming in summer would also have been easy, but a Korean in wet clothes or none at all would have been conspicuous.) Ethnic Koreans on the Chinese side of the border, descendants of people who had fled Korea during the Japanese occupation (1905-1945) could hide the North Korean refugees until they could make their way to a safehaven.

Qu drove us a kilometre downstream, where we walked to the summit of the restored Great Wall. On a North Korean island close to China, there was a cleared strip such as the one we had seen in 1999 along the Han River. From time to time, a North Korean soldier cycled along the strip. A Chinese telescope atop the Great Wall let us confirm that the cyclists were North Korean soldiers. That part of North Korea opposite Hushan appeared more prosperous than Sinuiju.

At the point where the Great Wall met the Yalu River, the Chinese had a museum. A bridge between the museum and the water had a bridge which led to the nearest North Korean island, but a barrier blocked the bridge, which was closed. The upper floor of the museum displayed replicas of the Terra Cotta monuments from Xian, China's capital during the Qin dynasty (221-206 BC), which had built the original Great Wall. There was even a statue of Shi Huangdi, the Qin (pronounced "Chin") emperor who had masterminded the building of the Wall erected to define China's border.

As we drove to our next destination, Fenguan Shan in the mountains north of Dandong, Qu continued to relate stories of North Korea. Chinese authorities, he said, had seized pictures taken by North Korean spies. North Korea's television sets offered only North Korean programmes. When Joan and I asked how residents of Sinuiju could be prevented from watching Dandong stations, there was no satisfactory answer. Hua, our interpreter, did not understand the question. Subsequently we learned that technicians could block the reception of selected channels.

Qu said that amputees could not enter Pyongyang. The North Korean capital was a showcase, and only healthy people could go there. When I asked how he could know that, Qu cited his former manager as a source. Moreover, said Qu, it was illegal to take cell phones to North Korea. (Cell phones were very popular in China.) Hua, born in 1968 when Mao's Cultural Revolution was in full swing but whose memories were those of his more tolerant successors, was shocked that North Koreans suffered from both hunger and thought control.

Qu indicated that there were not many defections, because the North Korean government took reprisals against families of defectors. One punishment, he said, was a ring through the nose, but Joan and I were not able to understand whether the punishment was reserved for unsuccessful defectors or for family members of successful escapees.

As we returned to Dandong, Qu suggested that Hua, Joan, and I dine at a North Korean restaurant. He passed one and left us at another. At both there were paintings of both the North Korean and Chinese flags above the door; these were the first North Korean flags which we had seen on Chinese territory. Hua explained that "special people" operated the restaurant, undoubtedly in order to earn money for the North Korean government. Joan suggested that the restaurant was a likely place for North Korean and Chinese businessmen to meet, and she overheard an English-language conversation between Asians at an adjacent table. Hua said that Qu had told her that waitresses (there were no waiters) could not walk Dandong's streets by themselves—only in groups. That way, even "special people" could observe each other. Hua advised us not to discuss

North Korea while inside the restaurant, as some of the North Korean staff might understand English.

The menu was available in Chinese and Korean, but not English, and included dog. There were no North Korean wines or beers, although Chinese varieties were available. The waitresses, all young and beautiful, were also singers and gave a superb concert to the largely male audience. Every waitress wore the North Korean flag, but not pictures of Kim Il Sung or Kim Jong Il. After a group of men left their table, the receptionist (who doubled as the lead singer) took broom and dustpan to clean their debris.

During breakfast the next morning on the 23rd floor of the Dandong International Hotel, we saw only one truck cross the Sino-Korean Friendshp Bridge. It was heading *into* North Korea. Joan and Hua said that while they watched North Korea the previous day by telescope from the Great Wall, they saw some eight to twelve women carry heavy sacks on their heads. Five tables from ours at breakfast, Hua noted three North Korean men. They had badges with pictures of Kim Il Sung.

The three of us returned to the Chinese shore of the Yalu River, where we found a North Korean store. We bought stamps and liquor. Then we had another motor boat ride. We saw a couple of civilians in Sinuiju who were riding bicycles, but no vehicular traffic. There was a truck, which was probably an army truck. Fishermen worked from the beach, not from boats. Sinuiju's buildings badly needed a coat of paint.

In the afternoon, we went to Dandong's Korean War Museum, formally known as the "Museum of the War against U.S. Aggression and in aid of Korea". Although the captions were recent, they reflected thinking of the 1950s, not of the 1990s and the 21st century.[9] Rather than admit, as Soviet documents and Soviet leaders have done, that the Korean War began when North Korea invaded South Korea 25 June 1950, the explanation was simply, "The war broke out." There was an exhibit devoted to the charge that the U.S. had resorted to biological warfare. A caption dismissed the demand of the United Nations Command that only those Prisoners of War who wanted to return to their country of origin should do so as a pretext to extend the fighting. Other exhibits admitted the role of the Soviet Air Force in fighting the war. The words "United Nations Command" and the acronym "UNC" always appeared inside quotation marks, and the impression was that the Chinese and North Koreans slaughtered UNC and

South Korean forces. There was a touching photo exhibit of some of the young Chinese men who had died for the cause.

Chinese tourists were visiting the museum in droves, and one looked at us as though to ask, "What are *you* doing here?" Joan and I were the only Occidentals there. One man who spoke English asked my thoughts on the exhibit. I mentioned their one-sidedness, especially the failure to admit that the war began when North Korea invaded South Korea. He agreed with me and questioned the credibility of everything there. "Yes, it *is* a bunch of lies. Doesn't it make you angry?"

That evening, as we dined again on the 23rd floor of the Dandong International Hotel, only the Chinese side of the Sino-Korean Friendship Bridge had lights, and we saw no traffic. There were a few lights in Sinuiju as we left the table, but only a few.

The next morning, Taxi Driver Qu drove us to our next destination, Changchun, capital of Japanese-occupied Manchuria (which they called "Manchukuo") and site of the court of the Emperor Pu Yi. Before we left, Hua told us that the television sets in our room provided access to channels from Hong Kong, Japan, even Taiwan, and *South* Korea, but not North Korea. Not surprisingly, the main story on the South Korean channel was the launching of the North Korean missiles, along with Japanese and U.S. reactions. Throughout breakfast, we saw no traffic on the Sino-Korean Friendship Bridge. As I paid the bill, Joan waited by the door. A man wearing a badge of either Kim Il sung or Kim Jong Il entered the hotel while she waited. Undoubtedly, he qualified as a "special person."

As we drove north, Qu told us that his paternal grandparents were Chinese who moved to Pyongyang and opened a restaurant there. Their son, Qu's father, was born there. Chinese people, said Qu, were free to leave North Korea and return to China, presumably because the North Korean government wanted good relations with China. Qu said that Chinese money was acceptable in North Korea, but that North Koreans could exchange money only on the black market.

Seeing North Korea across borders was not the same as visiting North Korea. Yet, we were probably more free to choose where we could go and what we would see than we might have been as part of a tour group visiting North Korea. Tourists could visit monuments and museums in Pyongyang and look out the train window as they travelled from Sinuiju to the capital, but we had a reasonable view of Sinuiju, its economy, and the people who live there, and of the North Korean borderlands upstream from Sinuiju. Hua and Qu were undoubtedly better guides than Kim Jong Il's paid professionals.

Note

1. 1. Bradley K. Martin, *Under the Loving Care of the Fatherly Leader: North Korea and the Kim Dynasty* (New York: St. Martin's, 2006). Martin interviewed many North Korean refugees who had fled to South Korea via China and a fourth country.

2. Jo Dong-ho, "Inter-Korean Rail Connection: Too Early to Get Excited", *Korea Focus*, XV, 2 (Summer 2007), pp. 10-12. Reprinted from *JoongAng Ilbo*, 21 May 2007.

3. Mtchell B. Lerner, *The Pueblo: A Spy Ship and the Failure of American Foreign Policy* (Lawrence: University Press of Kansas, 2002).

4. Jimmy Carter, *Beyond the White House: Waging Peace, Fighting Disease, Building Hope* (New York: Simon and Schuster, 2007), pp. 26-27 and 33.

5. *Shanghai Daily*, 20 June 2006.

6. *South China Morning Post* (Hong Kong), 17 June 2006.

7. Boutros Boutros-Ghali, *Unvanquished: A U.S.-UN Saga* (New York: Random House, 1999), pp. 126-127.

8. Boutros-Ghali, p.127.

9. The 2002 edition of *The Lonely Planet* (p. 407) indicated that captions would be in Korean and Chinese, but most of the Korean had disappeared and English-language signs were ubiquitous. From that, we deduced that the signs must have been fewer than five years old.

Chapter 12

The Thai-Cambodian Border

Almost everyone who has crossed the Thai-Cambodia border by land can report a scam in which he or she was involved. Joan and I, who made the trip in February 2008, are no exceptions. However, it is only fair to begin with a review of the area's recent history.

Thailand has—apart from violence related to its Muslim minority near the Malaysian border—enjoyed internal peace since 1945. It assisted the U.S. war effort in Vietnam, but the fighting took place elsewhere and Thailand benefitted from the spending of American money. Bangkok's traffic jams are notorious, and a recently built sky-train (which resembles its Vancouver counterpart) offers an escape. Bangkok's spanking new Suvarnabhumi International Airport is a regional hub, and Thailand's rail service puts Canada's to shame. Rich agricultural lands provide a wide range of food. Life expectancy is 70.2 for males, 75 for females. The literacy rate is 92.6 per cent.[1]

Cambodia, by contrast, has experienced a series of recent horrors.[2] A peace agreement arranged in Paris ended conflict among several Cambodian factions in 1991, but the most notorious—the Khmer Rouge—maintained enclaves until 1998. According to Professor Ben Kiernan of Yale University, one of the world's leading authorities on Cambodia, secondary school education was not available until 1933, and when the French left in 1953 there were only 144 high school graduates in the entire country. Enrolment in secondary schools was less than 3000, and there was no post-secondary education at all.[3] As they fought the Vietnam War for almost 13 years, U.S. forces quietly laid mines inside Cambodia near its border with Vietnam.[4] Later, the Khmer Rouge mined the border with

Thailand in order to prevent refugees from escaping.[5] The number of Cambodians missing one or more limbs (estimated at one of every 243 Cambodians in 1998) should shock even the most insensitive tourist.[6] The government of Canada, which played a leading role in outlawing the use of land mines by hosting the Ottawa Convention of 1997, has financed a horrendous land mines museum at Angkor Wat.

The Nixon administration continued to bomb Cambodia in 1973 for months after Secretary of State Henry Kissinger and North Vietnam's Le Duc Tho concluded "peace with honor" in January of that year.[7] U.S. destabilization of the country allowed the rebel Khmer Rouge regime to gain power 17 April 1975,[8] and before the Vietnamese army invaded Cambodia and ousted the Khmer Rouge in December 1978 and January 1979, at least 1.5 million of 7.9 Cambodians died.[9] Some died fighting the Vietnamese, with whom the Khmer Rouge had provoked a war, and others died of starvation, but hundreds of thousands died as a result of deliberate government policy. The Khmer Rouge executed members of ethnic minorities (Muslims, Chans, Vietnamese, Chinese), educated people and beneficiaries of pre-1975 Cambodian governments (whom they identified because they owned property, wore glasses, or spoke a European language), and political dissenters, even members of the Khmer Rouge who did not agree with current policy. Teachers and members of the Buddhist clergy were particularly vulnerable. Those who complained and those who inadvertently broke farm equipment with which they were working could suffer the death penalty, as could their families—even children and babies. One Cambodian taxi driver at Siem Reap who had a reasonable command of English and who came from an entrepreneurial family told Joan and me in 2007, during our first visit to Cambodia, that his family had survived the Khmer Rouge by hiding its knowledge. Pretending to know less than it did and playing dumb were the keys to survival. Many were less fortunate, and the deaths of so many educated people has cost Cambodia heavily in terms of development. Life expectancy for Cambodian males is 59.3, for women 63.4. The literacy rate is 73.6 per cent.[10] It is hardly surprising that some exploit opportunities at the Thai border in order that they may earn a somewhat decent living.[11]

Promptly at 7:30 a.m. on 30 January 2008, our minibus left Bangkok for the Thai-Cambodian border. There is train service between Bangkok and the Thai border community of Aranyaprathet, but when we enquired at Bangkok's

Hualamphong station, someone with a badge recommended that we do business with SK, a travel agency which had an office on the second floor. SK assured us that, unlike the railway which would stop at the border, it could take us all the way to Siem Reap.

Most of the highway from Bangkok to Aranyaprathet was four-laned and well paved. Crops of bananas, rice and sugar grew on prosperous-looking farms. At 11:45, the bus swung into a restaurant, where a man who introduced himself as a Cambodian distributed visa forms and offered to purchase our Cambodian visas for us.

There were problems. Joan and I had expected to purchase the visas in Cambodia, where we would pay in U.S. dollars. During our 2007 trip, when we had flown to Cambodia from Vietnam, we had learned that Cambodia used the U.S. dollar as *its* currency, and that Cambodian ATMs provide U.S. dollars to tourists with credit or debit cards. In 2007, we had purchased our Cambodian visas on arrival at Phnom Penh's airport. The Cambodian, whom I shall call Sherpa, told us that we must pay in Thai bahts, of which we had hardly any left. Sherpa warned that if we paid in dollars, we would face a delay of three days. He also warned that without his services, we would become part of a long line of people waiting to purchases visas inside the Cambodian border town of Poipet. Sherpa would spare us that agony by dealing with the Cambodian consulate in Aranyaprathet, and he promised to take us to an ATM for bahts. Indeed he did. Unlike any other ATM which we have experience in Thailand, previously or subsequently, the one which Sherpa used gave only two choices: 3000 bahts, or none at all. Sherpa said that the cost of a visa was 1200 bahts and that he charged an additional 100 for commission, but he helped himself to more than that. On 25 January 2008, the official exchange rate was 1000 Thai bahts for U.S. $32.21. The visas, once we had them, declared a face value of U.S. $20, approximately 650 bahts. Because Joan and I were a couple, we did not have as many surplus bahts as did people who were travelling by themselves.

After we cleared Thai Immigration, we walked across a bridge above a dried-up river into dusty, garbage-littered Poipet. From that point until Siem Reap, there were no paved roads. Casinos greeted new arrivals as we walked some 300 metres to the Cambodian immigration post. Sherpa explained that casinos were illegal in Thailand and that Poipet, like so many border cities in so many countries (including Canada), exploited the neighbours' weakness. At Immigration, there was a long line as officials photographed everyone of us. Nobody bothered to check the luggage.

Finally, a Cambodian bus transported us to a money changer who offered to change any surplus bahts. The rumour was that he helped himself to a 40 per cent commission. Joan and I asked about an ATM, but Sherpa said that there were not many in Cambodia. In his words, "Cambodia is not Thailand." We knew from experience that Cambodia does have ATMs and later discovered that they exist even in Poipet (at the ANZ bank). Finally, at 3:45 p.m., the bus left that unsightly and unattractive place.

The road from Poipet to Siem Reap was rough, to say the least. Both the type and quality of the road and the scenery reminded us of rural Saskatchewan during the late 1950s and early 1960s. Slash and burn farming was widespread, and the crops appeared thinner than in Thailand. Dust covered the banana leaves.

After a one-hour stop for supper, we resumed our seemingly interminable journey to Siem Reap, which finally arose like Las Vegas from the empty planes. However, instead of taking us to Old Market Square, as SK in Bangkok had indicated, the bus stopped at the Golden Mango Hotel. Another couple—two police officers from Montreal, Karen and Vincent—had reservations at Siem Reap's Ancient Angkor Hotel, as did Joan and I. However, the bus driver and the employees of the Golden Mango wanted us to stay there. Although we had paid no deposit, the four of us insisted that we had a moral commitment to the Ancient Angkor, and a taxi driver offered to take us there, for a price. We said that the Ancient Angkor had planned to fetch us at the Old Market Square, and that we must phone the Ancient Angkor. We had the number, but the Golden Mango official misdialled and let us hear a recorded message in Khmer and in English that no one was available. The official wanted us to believe that Reception at the Ancient Angkor had closed for the night. Karen, perhaps more suspicious than naïve professors because of the clientele which members of the Montreal police encounter on a daily basis, insisted that *she* must dial, and she all but grabbed the phone from the official's hand. Karen reached the Ancient Angkor's management without difficulty, and people from that hotel arrived within minutes to take us where we were supposed to go.

On 21 February 2008, a headline in Phnom Penh's English-language newspaper *Cambodia Daily* read, "Cambodia Most Corrupt Asian Nation: Group." Reporters Erika Kinetsz and Prak Chan Thul then explained that 75 per cent of Cambodians had bribed some official, usually a police officer or someone connected with the judicial system, within the past year. Of the 60 countries surveyed, only Cameroon, where 79 per cent claimed to have paid a bribe, was worse. It was hardly surprising. The Khmer Rouge destroyed the economy, but until 1991, non-Communist governments other than that of India rejected the successor government led by Hun Sen on the grounds that it was a puppet of the Vietnamese, who had invaded and imposed it. The genocidal Khmer Rouge, in the eyes of the world, was preferable to the Vietnamese, who had defeated the United States.[12] The wonder is that individual Cambodians are scrupulously honest. Apart from the border scam, which stretched from Aranyapraphet to the Golden Mango, no one tried to cheat Joan or me. Hotel operators, restauranteurs, merchants, and people in the transportation industry, had many opportunities to do so.

Notes

1. *World Almanac*, 2008, p. 834.

2. The best single summary of the horrors appears in William Shawcross, *Deliver Us from Evil: Peacekeepers, Warlords, and a World of Endless Conflict* (New York: Simon and Schuster, 2000), pp. 37-38, 49-59, 70-82.

3. Ben Kiernan, *Race, Power and Genocide in Cambodia under the Khmer Rouge, 1975-1979* (Chiang Mai, Thailand: Silkworm, 1997), p. 6.

4. Kiernan, p. 18. See also Purves, pp. 1-18, 42-54, 69-123.

5. Henry Kamm, *Cambodia* (New York: Arcade, 1998), p. 162.

6. Kamm, p. 15.

7. Kiernan, p. 20, Kamm, pp. 115-116.

8. See William Shawcross, *Sideshow: Kissinger, Nixon, and the Destruction of Cambodia* (London: Deutsch, 1979).

9. Kiernan, pp. 456-460. In their book, *Hun Sen, Strongman of Cambodia* (Singapore: Graham Brash, 1999), Marish C. Mehta and Julie B. Mehta estimate the death toll at 1.7 milllion; see pages 11 and 258. Kiernan does not disagree but chooses to err on the side of caution.

10. *World Almanac 2008*, p. 757.

11. Other useful books on Cambodia are Christopher Hudson, *The Killing Fields* (London: Pan, 1984); and Dith Pran (ed.), *Children of Cambodia's Killing Fields: Memoirs by Survivors* (Silkworm: Chiang Mai, 1997).

12. Mehta, pp. 125-151.

Chapter 13

The Border Between Hong Kong and the People's Republic of China

One of the world's most significant *internal* borders must be that between Hong Kong and the People's Republic of China (PRC). (As both North Korea and South Korea have been members of the United Nations since 1991, the inter-Korean boundary qualifies as "international.") Since the British mandate expired at the stroke of midnight 30 June/1 July 1997, Hong Kong has been a Special Administrative Region (SAR) of the PRC. Like Quebec and Ontario, which have different laws regarding, for example, language, education, and alcoholic beverages, Hong Kong and the PRC have different laws. The official language of the PRC is Mandarin, while Cantonese is widespread and has some legal status in Hong Kong. Chinese drive on the right, Hong Kongers on the left. Each has its own currency and postal system. When it comes to capital punishment, China ranks with Iran and the United States. Hong Kong has no capital punishment. Hong Kong's laws on spitting and smoking are stronger than those in the PRC, and while the PRC limits most families to one child, Hong Kongers are entitled to as many as they can support. Hong Kong's media are so outspoken that when the PRC banned foreign journalists from Tibet in March 2008, it also expelled those from its SAR, Hong Kong. International newspapers, magazines, and books are much more accessible in Hong Kong than in the PRC.

Differences between Hong Kong and the PRC are greater than those between Quebec and Ontario, and there certainly are no visible border controls between the two Canadian provinces. People travel freely from one to the other except when producers or vendors of beer or liquor in the one go on strike and thirsty consumers try to make purchases in the other. As they return to their province of origin, they may have to deal with the Sûreté du Québec or the Ontario Provincial Police, but such occasions are rare.

Officials of the State of California have routinely inspected incoming cars for fruit which might contaminate the California crop and removed oranges and grapefruit purchased elsewhere. However, passports are not required, nor are there exit controls. Anyone allowed to enter Nevada or Oregon is entitled to go to California, albeit without fruit.

The Hong Kong-PRC border is different, and movement from one side to the other presents challenges which North Americans do not have to face. Most visitors from Western countries need only a passport but no visa to enter and travel freely through Hong Kong, but those same people need a rather expensive visa, usually purchased at a Chinese consulate, in order to enter the PRC. As recently as March 2008, Dutch tourists reported that zealous PRC border officials had seized their copy of the tourists' Bible, *The Lonely Planet*. Conscientious officials in uniform scrutinize the passports of Hong Kong-bound travellers at Chinese airports, and of arrivals from Hong Kong when they land in the PRC. The border between Hong Kong and the PRC is porous, but its controls are tighter than those separating Canadian provinces or American states, let alone Australian states from each other or Scotland from England.

On 20 March 2008, Hong Kong's leading English-language newspaper, *The South China Morning Post* (which is as difficult to purchase inside the PRC as the U.S.-owned *International Herald-Tribune*) carried a story, which speaks volumes about Hong Kong-PRC relations. North of Sheung Shui, the 12th station on Hong Kong's Kowloon Canton Railway (KCR) from the southern terminus at Kowloon, the KCR divides. Some trains go northwest to Lok Ma Chau, and the rest go northeast to Lo Wu. North of Sheung Shui but throughout and south of Lok Ma Chau and Lo Wu, there is a "border zone," where casual travellers are not supposed to go and where Hong Kongers do not live. *South China Morning Post* reporter Denise Hung wrote that one Hong Kong official, Executive Councillor Leung Chung-ying, wanted to allow residents of the PRC to visit, study, and work in a "proposed border development zone" immediately south of the border. They would not need visas to go there. Inside that 20 square kilometre zone, Leung suggested to a radio audience, people from the PRC could benefit from Hong Kong's medical services. They could, with restrictions, perform certain types of work or attend specific schools. Councillor Leung's proposal reveals restrictions now in place at that border.

The previous day's *South China Morning Post* also illuminated the lack of mobility between the PRC and Hong Kong. On 18 March, Hong Kong's Court of Final Appeals informed 14 adults who had come to Hong Kong as children with their parents that they could not remain in the SAR. They must return to the PRC. The border between the PRC and Hong Kong really must be one of the world's tightest internal borders.

On 18 March 2008, I inspected the two Hong Kong border points opposite Shenzhen. The Shenzhen River separates Shenzhen from Lok Ma Chau and Lo Wu, and people on either side of the border benefit from the presence of the other. Shenzhen's Bureau of Trade and Industry advertises that city as "China's city of innovation" and cites "things you should know:

- Shenzhen's GDP ranks 4th among all cities of China.
- Shenzhen boasts the world's 4th largest container port.
- For the past 14 years, Shenzhen's exports have ranked 1st among all cities in mainland China.
- Of the Fortune 500 corporations, 146 currently have operations in Shenzhen.
- Shenzhen accounts for 40% of China's inventive patents.
- Since the mid-1990s, Shenzhen has focused on seven major industries, which include computer software, IT, and key projects of light industry and energy. The city's productive service industries, modern financial, modern logistics and modern culture sectors, are also highly advanced.
- The highly developed software and high-tech industries have laid solid foundations for Shenzhen's outsourcing businesses. Up till 2007, enterprises engaged in offshore outsourcing have been estimated to 100 with a total output of about 2.5 billion USD and 0.16 billion USD respectively in software and outsourcing export, accounting for 1/6 of the total.[1]

Shenzhen's skyline, clearly visible from Lok Ma Chau, reflects that prosperity, and the steady stream of trucks on the bridge which links the two communities and the six-lane highway from Kowloon to the bridge confirm that the PRC and Hong Kong, despite their differences, depend on each other. However, Lok Ma Chau and Lo Wu do not welcome casual visitors, as I was to discover.

The clean, ultra-modern Lok Ma Chau station at the northwestern terminus of the Kowloon Canton Railway (KCR) offered an unusual experience. The only ways out were to clear Hong Kong Immigration and proceed into the PRC, or else to take the smooth, rapid, KCR train back toward Kowloon. Most of the uniformed and non-uniformed people at the station could not speak English, but the few who did laughed when I said that I wanted to find a restaurant. I discovered a bakery, but consumption of food was illegal in the terminal and on the train, and lacking another PRC visa, I had no way out of the terminal except by train. Under the circumstances, I bought a croissant at the station's bakery and quickly stuffed it into my mouth, wondering for whose benefit the bakery was supposed to be operating.

The Shenzhen River is little more than the length of a football field in width, an easy swim. The Lok Ma Chau (Hong Kong) side appeared to be the underdeveloped shore. There were cranes which indicated considerable construction in Shenzhen, only wetlands on the south shore. Most passengers, perhaps all except those going to the PRC and myself, had left the train at the Sheung Shui.

Lo Wu is obviously a much more heavily traversed border crossing than Lok Ma Chau, but there was no way out of the station to go sightseeing, only to go to Shenzhen (assuming that one had the appropriate visa). Opportunities for taking pictures of Shenzhen were non-existent in Lo Wu, infinitely better in Lok Ma Chau. A family with small children had the same idea as mine, of seeing Lo Wu and then returning to Kowloon on a southbound train. That proved difficult. We could not leave the Lo Wu station and enter legally. An Information Officer advised us to go to the Arrivals (west) side of the platform and enter a coach as the other passengers were leaving. We had to be fast as the door would close and the southbound passengers would be boarding from the east side, to which we had no access. I asked about buying a ticket. The Information Officer said to use the ticket which had brought me from Lok Ma Chau to Lo Wu. I protested that I had not paid enough to cover the return trip to Tsim Sha Tsui, but he said not to worry. I could (and did) pay there.

In brief, Lok Ma Chau and Lo Wu are border crossing posts, not communities. Sheung Shui, less than an hour from Kowloon, is the most northerly population centre on the KCR.

Note

1. Advertisement on the back cover of *Beijing Review*, LV, 11 (13 March 2008).

Chapter 14

Money-Related and Other Problems

Some of the events cited here would not happen today in the era of ATMs, Visa, Mastercard, the Shengen Agreement, and the Euro (the common currency of most European countries in the 21st century). However, they *did* happen, and the developments noted in the previous sentence indicate something positive about the human race.

In August 1980, as we were leaving Zagreb to fly back to Toronto, Joe Konarek and I stood in line at Immigration. The line was long, and our wives decided to explore the terminal, then return as we approached the counter. Suddenly Joan and Barbara appeared. "Give us your surplus dinars!" they ordered as only professional teachers can do. "We found something to buy in one of the shops." Foolishly, we gave them our remaining dinars. Then, when we reached the counter, the Immigration Officer demanded that we pay a departure tax—in dinars. We explained that we no longer had any but could pay with travellers cheques. He demanded dinars, in cash. There was no choice but to leave the Immigration line, go to a money changer, then return to the Immigration line. By the time we cleared Immigration and reached the counter for seat assignment, which in those days could not be done on the internet, all the seats in the non-smoking section had been assigned. We non-smokers and anti-smokers had to sit in the smoking section not only across the Atlantic but over substantial portions of Europe and North America as well.

In August 1984, Joe and I flew from Frobisher Bay (now Iqaluit) on Canada's Baffin Island to Nuuk (formerly Godthaab), capital of Greenland, Danish territory. We entered the terminal and saw nobody in uniform. Most of the passengers simply walked out the door and onto the street, but we decided not to take chances. Might we have trouble leaving Greenland if we did not have an entry permit in our passports? Eventually we found an Immigration Officer and asked whether there were any entry formalities.

"Was that not a domestic flight?" he asked.

"No," we said. "We just arrived from Frobisher Bay."

"This is embarrassing," said the officer. "I thought that that was a domestic flight. So, let us say that I have given permission to everyone on that flight to enter Greenland."

In 1989, Joan, our son Andrew (age 11), and I travelled by train from Berlin to Goteborg, where we were to become proud owners of a car which we had ordered from a dealership in Ottawa. We left West Berlin, where we had been staying, with some West German Deutschmarks, crossed the Wall, and then took the train from East Berlin to Sassnitz, East Germany's port on the Baltic Sea. A Swedish ferry was waiting to transport us to Trelleborg. Based on experiences aboard North Sea ferries between the United Kingdom and The Netherlands, we assumed that there would be a *Bureau de Change* where we could purchase Swedish crowns. There was not. The cafeteria also made clear that it would not accept credit cards or change travellers cheques.

While I was pondering ways to finance the evening meal, I saw a series of what appeared to be laundry tubs. A boy stood facing the laundry tubs as coin after coin tumbled from the machine above. Suddenly I realized, "That boy is Andrew!" I raced forward, asked Andrew where he had found the money to put into the slot machine, and told him that we badly needed his earnings. He was not pleased, but I confiscated them nonetheless and promised to repay him the next day. A Swedish crown resembled a Canadian quarter in size, shape and value, and we paid for our dinner that evening in Swedish crowns, one at a time. The cafeteria cashier was not at all pleased, but what choice did we have?

From Trelleborg, the coach which we had originally boarded in East Berlin continued to Malmo, where we would spend the night. Alas! *The Bureau de Change* at the Malmo railway station had already closed for the night. We did not have enough crowns for a taxi, so I instructed Joan and Andrew to watch the luggage while I went for a walk in search of a hotel. I found one, but the receptionist would not accept either a travellers cheque or a credit card. He did agree that I could pay in West German Deutschmarks, at an extortionist rate of exchange, and given the options, I did so. By then, I had no Deutschmarks left. I returned to the station with the news. We used one of our few remaining crowns to rent space in a locker for whatever luggage we did not need that night, then walked as a threesome to the hotel.

Morning brought yet another problem. The *Bureau de Change* would open at 9 a.m., but our train left for Goteborg at 8:50. I took the remaining crowns to a bakery in the station, ordered two pastries, and gave the baker the last of our cash. He took pity upon us and added a third. Happily, that sustained us until Goteborg, by which time it was noon and the banks were open.

We took possession of our car in Goteborg, drove through Denmark and West Germany to Austria and Hungary, returned to Austria and proceeded to Switzerland, all the time letting our Austrian currency run down as we would need Swiss francs in Switzerland. We cleared Swiss Immigration without difficulty, but within seconds faced a challenge. The Swiss officer told us that in order to travel on an Autobahn (inter-urban highway), we must buy a permit. I explained that first we would have to purchase some Swiss francs, but there was no *Bureau de Change* or ATM.

"You must go to a bank," said the officer.

"Yes," I said, "but how will I go to a bank if I am not allowed to drive on a highway?" He did agree that that *was* a problem.

By good luck rather than by good management, we coped. The officer was willing to accept other Western European currencies. By combining our remaining Austrian, West German, Swedish, and Danish currency, the three of us had barely enough to pay for the permit. However, we did have enough and could proceed into Switzerland!

In 1992, Joan attended a conference for Commerce Professors (of which she was one) in Denmark. She then went to Zurich to visit her sister, and she did so on a Eurailpass—a kind of ticket which, if purchased outside Europe by a citizen of a non-European country, allows unlimited first class rail travel for a period of time on the railways of continental Western Europe. When she was crossing Germany on her return to Denmark for the return flight to Canada, she shared her compartment with a Yugoslav who had a fascinating, if tragic, story.

The man was an ethnic Croat and had been an employee of Yugoslav Rail. His career progress took him to a position in company headquarters, located in Belgrade, Serb capital and Yugoslavia's capital until its disintegration in 1991. With the secession of Croatia from Yugoslavia, the Serbs did not want him, but, he said, neither did the Croats. They were suspicious of someone who had lived in Belgrade. Under the circumstances, he sent his wife and children to live temporarily with his in-laws, then took advantage of the perk which came with Yugoslav Rail—a first class pass almost anywhere in Europe—to join his cousin in Sweden. His pass had not expired, and he hoped to re-establish himself there, then send for his family.

He left the former Yugoslavia with two suitcases, with a supply of U.S. dollars, the fruits of years of saving, in one of them. Suddenly, he came to a revolving door. He could not pass through the door carrying both suitcases and decided to take one, leave it outside, then return quickly for the other. Yet, in the brief period of time when the first suitcase was unattended, a thief grabbed it and disappeared. That was the suitcase with the U.S. money, and the man thought seriously of suicide.

Still with his pass, he headed north, toward the German-Danish border. Inside Germany, he met Joan and told her his story. At the border, they had to leave the train and walk to the other side. "You go first," he told Joan. "I am always a problem." Joan did as instructed, showed the outside of her Canadian passport to the Danish officer, who smiled and wished her a pleasant day. Then it was the Yugoslav's turn. Joan noticed that the smiling Danish officer suddenly changed into an officious bureaucrat. After some delay, the Yugoslav managed to persuade him that he would be Sweden's problem, not Denmark's, and the officer let him pass.

We wondered about the possible fate after the secession of Quebec of an English-speaking CN employee whose career progress had taken him from another province to company headquarters in Montreal.

Czechoslovakia dissolved into two countries at the stroke of midnight 31 December 1992/1 January 1993, and for some time, Slovakia developed a reputation for scams at the border. Joan and her brother Jim were victims of one such scam. In August 1994, they went to visit a common friend, Gabor Ruzskai, who had returned to Budapest after years of residence in Toronto. The three decided to take a train from Budapest through Slovakia and the Czech Republic to Vienna. At that time, Canadians did not need visas to go to Austria, but despite the end of the Cold War, they still needed them for Slovakia and the Czech Republic. Hungarians did not. Joan and Jim went to the Czech and Slovak Embassies in Budapest, the Hungarian capital, and purchased what the embassy staffs told them were the appropriate documents.

The outbound trip to Vienna was uneventful, as was the return trip through the Czech Republic. However, before they reached the Slovak-Hungarian border, a Slovak Immigration Officer approached them and asked to see their passports and visas. Joan and Jim produced them, but the officer was not satisfied. He said "Problem!" in English, then began a rant in what probably was the Slovak language. Finally Gabor, who knew some Slovak, told the officer that if they had the document which he wanted, they would have produced it, but they did not. Joan and Jim envisioned a scenario where they would have to leave the train before it exited Slovakia, and they asked Gabor to inform the Canadian Embassy in Budapest of their fate. Also, Gabor should telephone me back in Canada too.

Minutes before the train reached the border, the officer returned and literally threw the two passports at Joan and Jim. Clearly he was angry, perhaps because they had not offered him a bribe. Hungarian officers aboard the train watched the entire performance, and once the train was inside Hungary, they approached Joan and Jim with huge smiles. "Normally," they said, "we request a Hungarian visa surcharge at this point, but in your case, we shall not do so." Gabor explained that Hungarians and Slovaks felt longstanding animosity against each other, in large measure because of conflicting territorial claims. The Hungarians were undoubtedly pleased that Joan and Jim had not given any money to the Slovak.

Significantly, the European Union demanded greater integrity in government before it would admit Slovakia into full membership. Slovakia became a member of the EU in 2004.

Conclusions

Canadians are very fortunate. Yes, some Canadian Customs and Immigration Officers can be officious and legalistic to the point of foolishness. Yes, Canadian fishermen do from time to time fish illegally in U.S. waters and clash with authorities on the other side of the border.[1] However, most officers within Canada and in the three countries on Canada's borders—the United States, France (St. Pierre et Miquelon), and Denmark (Greenland)—are highly professional people of integrity, and border violations are not lethal. Thanks to these people, undesirable people and harmful commodities remain at a distance, and exotic animals and birds can freely live in jungles instead of caged in somebody's living room, or face an even worse fate.

Canadians have as much freedom to travel as any human beings. Unlike the governments of North Korea and the former East Germany, the government of Canada does not restrict the right of Canadians to visit foreign countries. Unlike people with British passports, problems related to the disintegration of empire and decolonization have not made Canadians unwelcome. Unlike Americans, whose government forbids unauthorized travel to Cuba and certain other countries, we Canadians can go where we please as long as the host country will admit us.

Also important is the sense of accommodation. Both Canadians and the immediate neighbours—Americans, Danes, and French—have long accepted the location of the land borders. (Hans Island, between Ellesmore Island and Greenland, remains in dispute, but it is small, uninhabited, and remote.) Scholars on both sides of the Canada-U.S. boundary have argued that their side was short-changed in some of the 18th and 19th century boundary settlements, and tiny Point Roberts south of Vancouver, located at the tip of a peninsula isolated from the rest of the United States, was certainly a product of indifference or ignorance on the part of the diplomats who placed the border where it is. St. Pierre et Miquelon may strike some Canadians who are aware of its existence as a quaint anachronism, and enforcement of the Danish-Canadian border between Greenland and Ellesmere Island once interfered with the lifestyle of nomadic Inuit who had lived in the area for millennia.[2] However, Canada's borders have been in place for so long that almost everyone agrees that changes would create more problems than solutions. Canadians, and the neighbours of Canadians, have accepted the status quo in a way that many in Ireland have not. Unlike residents of Northern Ireland before the Good Friday settlement of 1998, Canadians and Canada's neighbours need not live in fear of violence launched from the other side of the border, a factor which enhances the quality of life.

Prosperity is a big asset. Despite pockets of poverty, Canada and its three neighbours are prosperous countries. Citizens of each can reasonably hope to live well without going where they are not wanted. Some do work illegally in other countries, but not many and not for long. Job security at home is usually preferable to possible deportation and the uncertainties of ongoing employment. North Koreans and even some Trinidadians are willing to gamble, even with their lives, in ways that Canadians, Americans, Danes, and French citizens need not.

Section I confirms that establishing boundaries requires effort. Iceland succeeded in what it attempted; the jury remains out with regard to Chile's claims in Antarctica and the problems involving Trinidad and Tobago with its neighbours. Since 1980, Yugoslavia has disintegrated, and travelling from one part of it to another has become considerably more difficult than it was then. Romania is a candidate for the Schengen Agreement, whereby since 1985 most of continental Europe's countries outside the former Soviet Union, as well as Iceland, have abolished border controls and accepted common rules about people who arrive from elsewhere. Canadians have little difficulty at border crossings in Latin America, except for such challenges as the Costa Rican-Panamanian crossing at Paso Canoas, where the international bus drops passengers on one side and meets them on the other. At that chaotic crossing on the Pan American Highway, inexperienced passengers really do need someone to guide them. The Inter-German border has disappeared, and both Austria and Hungary have joined the Schengen Accord. Although both the United Kingdom and the Republic of Ireland remain aloof from Schengen, they have a Schengen-like accord with each other. Since the return of peace to Northern Ireland with the Good Friday Accord of 1998, the inter-Irish border is as open and demilitarized as those separating one continental Schengen country from another.

Zimbabwe and North Korea remain trouble spots, but, despite its challenges, the Thai-Cambodian border *is* open—in contrast to the situation when the Khmer Rouge had power. Whether it will remain open is unclear. As this manuscript goes to press (October 2008), Thai and Cambodian soldiers face, and even shoot each other, near the Preah Vihear archaeological site, where both countries have claims. For the foreseeable future, the border between Hong Kong and the People's Republic of China is likely to retain its unique position as the world's most closely monitored *internal* border.

A peaceful border which we can cross at will and undesirables do not is a factor which Canadians take foregranted. A look around the world reveals that such is not a universal reality. Yet, the situation has improved since the events discussed in the final chapter. Perhaps the world is headed in the right direction after all.

Notes

1. See, for example, the story of the *Last Time*, a fishing boat based at Sault Ste. Marie, Ontario, in Graeme S. Mount, John Abbott, Michael J. Mulloy, *The Border at Sault Ste. Marie* (Toronto: Dundurn, 1995), pp. 69-70.

2. Trevor Lloyd, "Grønlandsk-canadiske forhold," *Grønland*, XXVI, 5 (June 1978).

Index

Also by Graeme S. Mount

CHILE AND THE NAZIS: From Hitler to Pinochet
Graeme S. Mount

Based on documentary evidence from the archives of the Chilean Foreign Office, and from U.S., British, German, and, intercepted, Japanese documents, Mount is one of the first authors to provide evidence of Chile's reluctance to sever diplomatic ties with Nazi Germany allowing Nazi Germany to maximize its opportunities there, influencing Chilean politicians, military operations, and the popular media.

> Mount's cool, clear prose avoids the expressions of outrage that blunt so many books about the Right in Chile. His revelations are enough. Highly recommended. —*The Guardian*

> A most impressive book, based on a variety of archival and oral historical sources from three continents. —Stan Hordes, University of New Mexico

> Reveals the conflict, espionage, and difficulty with policy which resulted from widespread Nazi influence. —Florentino Rodao, Asociacion de Estudios del Pacifico

2001: 204 pages, paper 1-55164-192-5 $19.99 ✳ cloth 1-55164-193-3 $48.99

THE DIPLOMACY OF WAR: The Case of Korea
Graeme S. Mount, with Andre Laferriere

In 1950, North Korea invaded South Korea. Sixteen nations fought on behalf of South Korea; two (the People's Republic of China and North Korea itself) on behalf of North Korea. By the time the fighting stopped, nearly two million military, and an estimated three million civilians, had lost their lives, with one-half of Korean industry, and one-third of Korean homes destroyed. For two of the three years that the war was under way, both sides were trying to negotiate a peace.

> The great strength of the book is in the wealth of detail with which Mount charts the course of policy-making. Fifty years on, the relationship is as relevant as ever. —Peter Londey, Historian, Australian War Memorial, Canberra

> Interesting, readable, and exceedingly well documented. —John Melady, *Korea: Canada's Forgotten War*

> Both assesses previous histories and presents its own judicious findings...makes complex diplomatic history accessible. —Hank Nelson, Australian National University, Canberra

ANDRE LAFERRIERE teaches history at the William G. Davis Sr. Public School in Brampton, Ontario.

2004: 224 pages, paper 1-55164-238-7 $24.99 ✳ cloth 1-55164-239-5 $53.99

Also by Graeme S. Mount

895 DAYS THAT CHANGED THE WORLD: The Presidency of Gerald R. Ford
Graeme S. Mount, with Mark Gauthier

Making extensive use of the Gerald Ford Presidential Library, *895 Days* examines the very documents produced by President Ford, members of his cabinet, and the White House staff and through that examination offers a window on the world between August 1974 and January 1977.

> A refreshingly candid picture of a dramatic two and one half year period in America's history. From the highs, to the lows, the authors are not afraid to praise and condemn. —Edelgard E. Mahant, York University.

> Graeme Mount's books and articles are known for their rich detail and clear conclusions, and this work detailing Gerald Ford's foreign policy is no exception...a thoughtful analysis by a person who understands the United States, but can also maintain a dispassionate perspective. —John Bratzel, Michigan State University

MARK GAUTHIER, who holds an MA in history from Laurentian University, has also written about Canadian-Cuban relations in the era of Diefenbaker and Kennedy.

2005: 240 pages, paper 1-55164-274-3 $24.99 ✳ cloth 1-55164-275-1 $53.99

---

send for a free catalogue of all our titles

C.P. 1258, Succ. Place du Parc
Montréal, Québec
H2X 4A7 Canada

or visit our website at http://www.blackrosebooks.net

to order books

In Canada: (phone) 1-800-565-9523 (fax) 1-800-221-9985
email: utpbooks@utpress.utoronto.ca

In United States: (phone) 1-800-283-3572 (fax) 1-651-917-6406

In UK & Europe: (phone) London 44 (0)20 8986-4854
(fax) 44 (0)20 8533-5821 email: order@centralbooks.com

Printed by the workers of
for Black Rose Books

imprimerie **gauvin**
